AF317001

ON HANDS AND KNEES

The Meaning of Life and Adventures from Four Generations

Charles K. Abel

Contents

The Meaning of Life

From Four Generations

This book is a series of stories covering 140 years and four generations, a famous Reverend, two Knights of the Realm and a Deputy Prime Minister.

The setting is from the streets of 19th Century London, to the Kauri gum forests of New Zealand to the islands and mountains of Papua New Guinea.

The author, Charles Kauvu Abel, is the great grandson of the pioneer missionary, Reverend Charles William Abel of the London Missionary Society, and former Deputy Prime Minister, Treasurer and Planning Minister, and three-term parliamentarian.

He recounts a dramatic history, love story, enduring faith and joy in family, music, and sports.

A remarkable journey of discovery about the meaning of life!

Dedication

To my dear father, my two grandfathers, my great grandfather, and the country to which they were committed.

A sincere thank you to my best friend, Hacy, and our children, Nikita, Courtney, and Jordan, (and bubu Aaliyah), for your love and patience.

CKA

Preface

Four Generations, a family history and personal memoir by Charles K. Abel is a moving tribute to the author's distinguished patrilineage and to his father, Chris Abel, who passed away in December 2022. Significantly, this publication is an invaluable contribution to Papua New Guinea's rich oral and written history, which continues to branch out like the boughs of a tree, interconnecting the lives of diverse tribes and foreigners in both conflict and spiritual communion.

The history of the Abel family tree is well-known in Milne Bay Province. It is a story of *"taim bilong tumbuna ikam long tete"*. *Four Generations* expands on this history by drawing on archives, letters, previously published work, and the family stories that have been passed down from father to son. In a fast-paced readable narrative, with thrills and fears of tribal warfare and white man's war, and interspersed with the humanity and compassion of the Abel family's mission, Charles Abel Jr. brings to life key moments in Papua New Guinea's colonial and missionary history.

The publication revisits several colonial atrocities, including the brutal expeditionary force in 1903 in the Paiwa area, which is now part of the Rabaraba District, and how Charles Abel Senior intervened and sought reconciliation and peace with the Paiwa people. It also revisits his protests concerning the use of force and firearms as the means of 'pacification' at Goaribari, which led to a Royal Commission of Inquiry.

The publication also recounts the missionary expedition undertaken by Charles' Grand Uncle, Cecil Abel, to the Kunika part of the mountainous Owen Stanley range in 1935, where he risked being murdered by the 'natives'. Instead, he chose to camp with them and eat with them, convincing his tribal adversaries that he was not like other white people, but was a friend.

Through this personal memoir, the author continues the family legacy of dedication, adventure, and commitment to nation building. As a young man, Charles K. Abel traversed the Highlands of Papua New Guinea, working as a chief financial officer for a private company. He gained leadership experience to become a competent politician and Minister of State, and developed innovative policies to guide Papua New Guinea's future development. Also, as an accomplished musician, Abel is one of the current generation of Papua New Guineans who knows the value of keeping history alive and who is determined to add value to the quality of life in Papua New Guinea, from what was planted in the ground by his forebears.

Sir Charles W. Lepani

Chapter 1

A Short Ride

"I just want you to know that I love you, Dad"

"I love you too, Charlie", was the soft reply, and the last coherent words to me from my father.

I dedicate this memoir to my father, my formidable great grandfather and grandfathers, and the indomitable spirit of love and service that they exemplified.

I want to take you on **a short ride through four generations of stories** in the hope that you can be entertained and moved in a small way. It would be my absolute privilege to maybe add something of value to your life!

My great grandfather begins this journey as a London boy, who set off to New Zealand at 19 years of age, in 1881. He found his calling while living amongst the Maoris, learning their language, praying with them, and defending them.

He returned home to attend Cheshunt College, and as Reverend Charles William Abel of the London Missionary Society, he was diverted from his original intentions to return to New Zealand. Instead, he chose the relatively new field of British New Guinea, to which he sailed in 1890.

He built one of the most successful industrial missions of the day, based on Kwato Island, Milne Bay, at the eastern tip of the mainland of Papua New Guinea, and left an indelible legacy of **faith, service, hard work, music, and cricket.** The **love story** between he and his wife, Beatrice, whom he met on the journey by ship from London to Sydney, is one that lasted a lifetime.

These are themes that resonate throughout this book and four generations, up to today.

I write of the Paiwa Massacre, the Goaribari Affray, and suicide of Christopher Robinson, the survival of an ambush, and the sacrifice of a first-born daughter in the chapter, **"Blessings and Burdens"**.

My grandfathers, (Sir) Cecil and Russell Abel, seemed to have little choice in their destiny to continue the 'great work' and they did so with the same dedication as their father. They were both Cambridge educated anthropologists and gifted writers, thankfully, leaving works behind that we can draw upon today.

Cecil was the charismatic elder brother who inspired a spiritual revival in a disheartened church, following the death of his father in 1930. His time was not without controversy when he left Kwato in 1951, but he would go on to make a significant contribution to the war effort, and in politics and the independence movement of the fledgling nation of Papua New Guinea. He was knighted in 1982. I write of these efforts in the chapters, **"Monster on the Horizon"**, and **"We the People"**.

Russell's leadership of the church ushered in a period of thirteen years of stability and consistency. He was the quieter of the two brothers, with an artistic flair and was much loved by everyone who knew him. He died on a medivac flight out of Kupiano, Abau District, after being carried on a stretcher for sixteen hours from Amau Village, where the Kwato Church had built a mission.

I write of the Kunika expedition by Cecil, following a request by the Lieutenant Governor, Sir Hubert Murray, and followed up by Russell, to try to tame the dreaded inland Abau people, in 1934 (leading to the establishment of the mission at Amau), in the chapter, **"Wallaby Country"**.

Russell and Cecil's marriages were also wonderful love stories, and I have fond memories of (Lady) Semi (Bwagagaia) Abel, and Ruth Sheila (Porteous) Abel. Our grandmother, Sheila, was a kind and gentle lady who took care of my two brothers and I during our high school days on the Sunshine Coast, Queensland.

My father, (Sir) Christopher Abel, was born in a snowstorm in Dunedin, New Zealand, during the Second World War. He returned to Kwato Island at five years of age and spent seven years there, before going back to Australia for further education. He spoke fluent Suau (language) all his life, and published the Suau Dictionary in 2013.

He came back to Papua New Guinea in 1963, as an agricultural officer and spent time in the Mekeo area of Central Province, where he met my mother, Barbara (Kauvu) Abel. He spent time at Kokoda before going home to Milne Bay, where he made a tremendous contribution in the private sector, to the landowners, and to the Kwato Church. He was knighted for his services in 2018.

I will forever carry in my heart his profound example of love and dedication. Was it all smooth sailing? Certainly not. I write of some of our childhood trauma in the chapter, **"During a Snowstorm"**, and other adventures from his time in the chapters, **"Two Plane Crashes"**, and **"Rich Harvest"**.

Despite growing up with some privileges, I had the feeling of somehow being poor compared with the 'neighbours', and combined with my childhood experiences, I had a sense of insecurity as I went forth.

We were called the 'caramel kids' (because of our colour) and people used to snicker and talk about my parents' domestic problems.

This drove me towards certain selfish behaviour as a response, including the perception that making money was the answer. I would find in wealth acknowledgement and happiness.

I write about some of the lessons that I learned about money through my father's example and my experiences through the surfing days in high school, university, and the early working days after university, in the chapter, **"Caramel Kids"**.

I've basically trained five to six days a week since Grade 8 or Grade 9, such is my love for the discipline and meditational experience of hard physical work and exercise. In the chapter, **"Running for No Reason"**, I write of health and fitness, and my obsession, including time on the bodybuilding stage, diet, and sleep, and a time when people laughed at why we were lifting weights. Today, weight training and fitness saturates the social media and modern competitive sports and lifestyles.

Another theme is the passion for music. Charles William Abel introduced the Tonic Solfa music system to Papua and Kwato was renowned for its harmonious and enthusiastic singing of praise.

Dad made us coconut ukuleles, and I would immerse myself in his music record collection after school, using the old turntable record player.

I was in a popular high school singing group, and my brother, Owen, and I began thrashing around in bands on the university holidays.

The chapter, **"Coconut Ukulele"** is about this experience and my band the Wabo Knights, with three albums and two national Number One songs.

When I went to work in Mendi in the Southern Highlands Province, as the manager for Kiburu Lodge, I was introduced to a more intense, violent environment, and a beautiful and strong people in the inhabitants of the mountains. I went on to become financial controller for the parent company, Global Constructions, and learned so much from my bosses and these proud people. I describe this in the chapter, **"Another Planet"**.

I was financial controller for a trucking company that was owned by the Ipili Porgera landowners, based in Lae City. We were responsible for making sure that 240 000 litres of fuel reached the Porgera Gold Mine every day, along one of the toughest roads in the world – the 800 kilometre Highlands Highway. I write of the demands of expatriate bosses, who were on 'fly-in-fly-out' rotation, endless compensation the highway drivers and wonderful people of Lae and the Highlands Highway in the chapter, **"A Trucking Life"**.

I owe much of the lessons of my life to my wife and best friend, Hacy Henao Abel. I emphasize a major theme of this book in the centrality of family and marriage in the chapter, **"The Queen"**.

The chapters, **"I Need My Son"**, and, **"On Hands And Knees"**, concern my 'accidental' entry into national politics and my time as the local Member of Parliament for the Alotau Open Electorate, where I served for three terms.

Ever since I can remember, I have had the unfortunate ability to see and feel certain things of a supernatural nature. This intensified when growing up at KB Mission where many soldiers from both sides were killed during the Second World War.

On the campaign trail in my first election, in 2007, I had perhaps the most disturbing experience of my life, from a visitor in the night. It has very much helped to shape my beliefs regarding the spiritual journey that I describe throughout the book. That chapter is called, **"The Witch"**.

In the chapter, **"Reaching for the Stars"**, I write of my time as the Minister for National Planning and Monitoring, and the thoughts behind the National Strategy for Responsible Sustainable Development (StaRS), the Medium-Term Development Plan 2, and the *National Planning and Monitoring Act*, that I initiated.

When I was the Minister for Treasury and Deputy Prime Minister, we undertook our country's first-ever sovereign bond issue, including a roadshow around the world in eight days. I nearly killed myself, but the result was a three times oversubscription, and three international awards. This chapter is called, **"Eight Days"**.

Papua New Guinea is incredibly endowed with natural resources, yet we remain so poor. I begin this discussion and strategy to overcome this problem in, **"Reaching for the Stars"**. In the chapter, **"So Much Gold"**, I delve more into the issue of our non-renewable resources and their proper management, including my experience in the negotiations of the US$ 13 billion Papua LNG Project, the US$ 6 billion Wafi-Golpu Project, and the renegotiations of the Porgera Gold Mine fiscal terms, as Treasurer.

The chapter, **"It Does Not Belong to You"**, contains my thoughts on what constitutes genuine leadership, and how it applies at all levels. I write of some of the political history in the formation of the National Governments in 2011, 2012, and 2017.

The final chapter, **"The Meaning of Life"**, crystalizes all of the lessons from four generations of service to this country, Papua New Guinea. It unlocks the secret to a successful life (well, just my humble interpretation anyway).

"If you direct your thoughts and control your emotions, you will ordain your destiny." Napoleon Hill

"God declares, I think of you and I have plans for you, prosperity and a future filled with hope." Jeremiah 29:11

Charles K. Abel

Chapter 2

Blessings and Burdens

"Evangelical missionary activity in the Western Pacific reached a climax in the career of Charles William Abel (1862 – 1930). His long lifespan, the remarkable range of his interests, the sustained energy of his ambitions, all gave his work a significance unrivalled by that of any other single missionary." **(Wetherell, David. "Charles Abel – The Kwato Mission of Papua New Guinea 1891 – 1975", 1996, p xi).**

Resident Magistrate of the newly established North-East Division, Charles Arthur Whitmore Monckton, and his contingent of forty Papuan constabulary, mainly Orokaivans, including Sergeants Barigi and Oia, had made their way carefully by two oar boats to the shore several hundred metres to the south of Giwa Village of the Paiwa language zone. It was early March 1903, and several hours before dawn.[1]

Monckton was determined to teach these people a proper lesson following reports of the murder of a mixed race, West Indian trader named Jackson. The Paiwa people were constantly raiding their neighbours and the Anglican Church had complained several times about the inaction of the government.

Monckton was quite proud of his reputation as a hard-nosed disciplinarian, and professed a 'shoot and loot' approach to troublesome natives in his later writings. He was born in New Zealand and had been a trader in British New Guinea, before applying for an appointment in the administration in 1897. He knew exactly from his experience of the Maoris in New Zealand, that disobedient natives knew only tough justice. On this occasion, he was particularly keen to see how the use of bayonets could be used in an arrest.

He gathered the team together on the beach and instructed that bayonets, which had been sharpened on the ship ride from Cape Nelson, should be fixed, and no shooting was allowed. All the village men were to be gathered in the centre of the village at gunpoint. He made it quite clear that any resistance whatsoever was to be met with violent force.

All were on full alert as they crept up to the village, as these were people of a fierce reputation. In the early light of dawn, they discovered a quiet village completely unaware of any prospective raid upon them.

---

[1] *There is a contradiction of sorts as to this timing in Monckton's own report, where he describes an afternoon raid. However, his past punitive raids clearly indicate a preference of attacking in the early hours while the village sleeps.*

With the village surrounded, several mangy dogs had begun to bark urgently. Monckton hurriedly had Sergeant Barigi call out in the Police Motu language several times, that the village was under arrest for the murder of trader Jackson, and that all of the men were to come out and stand in the middle of the village immediately.

As faces began to emerge from the doorways, there were several cries of consternation and fear and general chattering and hubbub. A child began to scream and cry. Gradually, the men began to materialize and gather and the constabulary squeezed in closer. A commotion suddenly developed to Monckton's right, when he heard a shot go off and yelled, "Use your bayonets you bastards!" He could barely suppress his surge of excitement.

There was a melee, with people generally scattering in all directions, and making to get out of the village, screaming, and dogs barking. There were around twenty unarmed village men trapped in the vortex, and as they attempted to flee, the policemen dived upon them, stabbing indiscriminately with the ends of their rifles.

"Shit, shit, shit!!" Monckton swore as the scale and repercussions were realized in his clouded mind. He composed himself as he heard a female shriek break the morning air, and staggered over to the village centre. There were 18 bodies there, and several police were still stabbing at some of them. He suspected some tribal enmity was motivating the mutilation and ordered them to stop.

There was jostling and screaming continuing from one of the huts, and he discovered three prone naked village girls, and ten policemen pinning and raping them in turns. He watched the scene for several minutes before declaring, "Hurry up, we have work to do!"

The south coast of Makamaka is of minimal soil on hard limestone and coral. Monckton ordered that chunks of coral be tied to the bodies and thrown in the sea. After washing off the gore, the party with seven bound male prisoners made their way back to the oar boats. They burned all the houses and shot any pigs and dogs in the vicinity. All others had disappeared except for the three sobbing ladies.

It was found in the court hearings conducted in June of the same year by the Chief Judicial Officer, and Acting Administrator for Papua, Christopher Robinson, that the supposed victim, in whose name the punitive expedition was undertaken, was alive and well. Regardless, he sentenced one of the villagers to fourteen years hard labour, and the others to seven years for attempted murder. A further glaring anomaly was that he never called on him (Jackson) to appear at the hearings.

When further evidence emerged of the rapes by the constabulary, Robinson was compelled to reopen the case resulting in the mere dismissal of two policemen, with a fine of two pounds each.

It was the 4th of March 1904, and the fresh-faced Christopher S. Robinson was standing at the bridge of the 147-foot, 170-ton *Merrie England*, with the prevailing north-westerly monsoon winds of the Gulf of Papua filling the sails above him. His chest swelled as he surveyed his domain on this Western District inspection. He was the first Australian appointed to the role of Administrator (Acting) over the former Protectorate of British New Guinea, and was only 32 years old. His substantive position was Chief Judicial Officer, and in his starched whites with his Commandant WC Bruce, 39 Armed Native Constabulary, and a host of other administrative subordinates on board, he felt very much in control of his destiny.

It was time to sweep out the British colonial vestiges and its feeble patronage, and establish a new order under the Australian Commonwealth. Robinson was convinced that his predecessor, Le Hunte, had been too lenient in the handling of the Goaribari Affray, and as such, the murderers of London Missionary Society (LMS) missionaries, Reverends James Chalmers and Oliver Tomkins were still at large. The skull of Tomkins had not been recovered even after three years. Matters of recalcitrant natives had to be dealt with swiftly and decisively. This was his moment to establish a reputation, impress the Prime Minister, and secure the role as Lieutenant Governor.

Goaribari Island was just coming into view on the Eastern horizon. Robinson had managed to keep the whole operation rather vague and the Commandant still remained concerned at the lack of a coherent strategy, and he had expressed this to Chief Operating Officer Rothwell, and Resident Magistrate Jiear. He understood they were to make some arrests relating to the 1901 murderers of Chalmers and Tomkins and their local party. He and Jiear had related several concerns to the Administrator, including the risks of trying to effect an arrest on board, rather than onshore, and the bad precedent it would set, as far as building trust with the natives for the future.

Of further concern to Bruce was the relative inexperience of half of the constabulary, who were new recruits, and that many of them were from the Daru and Kiwai Islands. A Chief Navagi and some of the missionary students who had been killed and eaten in the Goaribari Affray were Kiwai Islanders.

Captain Harvey had pulled Bruce aside the day before and informed him of the direct instructions from Robinson that the mounted Nordenfelt machine gun was to be loaded and ready at all times. In response, the Commandant had advised his sergeants to order all troops not to engage or fire upon any villagers unless the orders came directly from him.

There was a deep sense of foreboding as they dropped anchor off Dopima Village on the northern shore of Goaribari Island, opposite Omati River on the mainland. On the following morning, being Saturday the 5th of March, there was little initial movement from the shore. Gradually, a canoe approached and an interpreter explained to the inquirer that it was the government delegation passing through, and they were happy to trade with the people and extended an invitation for them to approach the ship. It was historical practice that punitive expeditions always involved disembarkation and a shore-based interaction, so it was reassuring to the people when this did not initially occur. It wasn't long before there was quite a gathering of canoes and exchange of tobacco, axes, yams, and even bows and arrows taking place.

Robinson maintained his distance, but was able to ascertain through some of the senior policemen that Lake' and Emma, two of the primary culprits, were in the crowd. They had quickly disappeared though, and the day concluded without incident.

The following day, being Sunday the 6th of March, drew a huge crowd from the outset. There were a least 600 people eventually congregated around the *Merrie England* in all shapes of canoes, and even a crowd on deck.

At around midday, it was whispered to Robinson that Lake' was on deck and Emma was in a canoe below. He summoned Jiear to his cabin and ordered him to prepare to arrest Lake' and Emma and those around them. The Magistrate made a last appeal for reconsideration, but to no avail. As he left, he noticed Robinson loading his Martini Henry rifle.

Robinson was actually terrified, but he was not showing it. He dried his sweaty hands off, steeled himself and waited. It wasn't long before he heard a senior sergeant announce, "..arrest!" interspersed with the Motu language and he sprang up to the deck, suddenly feeling more alive than ever before.

The sergeant had a revolver to the head of Lake' and he and eight others were surrounded by the constabulary, with rifles aimed at them. Naturally, all the other visitors panicked and went tumbling and diving overboard. As the arrested realized the moment and made to escape, Bruce screamed, "No shooting!!" and they began clubbing them with their rifle butts.

He suddenly heard a shot explode from the upper deck and turned to see Robinson shooting down to the canoes and yodelling, "Arrows turned on us! Fire at will, fire at will!!"

Captain Harvey and the gunner crew let loose with the Nordenfelt creating a deafening roar, and the constabulary who had been restraining themselves with great difficulty, now shot a couple of the unarmed prisoners then opened fire on the canoes.

Bruce took a moment to realize what was happening before racing to the Administrator's position and surveying the carnage below him. There was no sign of any arrows coming from below. Under such withering fire it was just a scene of capsized canoes and people swimming in all directions or in various stages of death throes, thrashing about or floating on the surface. He wrestled the rifle out of the hands of Robinson who seemed in a completely frenzied state. Running back to the others it took him some yelling and slapping of faces to stop the shooting.

In only two minutes of combined fire, 300 rounds had been dispersed, sixty people killed, and unknown numbers injured.

It was the early hours of an already warming morning in the dusty colonial outpost of Port Moresby on the 20th June 1904. Christopher S. Robinson, 32 years of age, but looking weathered and tired stood with slumped shoulders before his administration building. His glazed eyes were oblivious to the first stirrings of the village and colonial life around him. He was two hours earlier than usual. A fly buzzed around his stained white collar, and after an eternity, settled on the edge of his moustache. The Chief Judicial Officer and Acting Administrator of the Territory of Papua fell to his knees at the foot of the naked flagpole. His lips seemed to be mumbling an incoherent prayer, and a tear squeezed its way and rolled down his cheek. In a surprisingly swift moment, he drew a revolver from his coat, thrust the barrel into his chin, and shot himself through the jaw and out the top of his head.

500 kilometres away to the east, on Kwato Island, the Reverend Charles William Abel (Abel) received the news several days later. Naturally, it had caused a sensation, particularly on Samarai Island, the second largest settlement in British New Guinea, now the Territory of Papua. Abel had to consciously pause the torrent of ramifications that welled and exercise a prayer. He had only recently recovered from the malaria fever. His eyes turned once again to the soothing hilltop view across the narrow blue strait to Logeia Island.

These were turbulent days and eruptions from a running battle he was having since he had returned from his first ten-year furlough leave under the LMS. The more cordial times under the British Administrators of Sir William MacGregor and Sir George Le Hunte, it seemed, were over. Their sympathetic views of the work of the missions and the benevolent attitude of an aged and apparently wiser colonial master had been taken for granted.

The Australians were being handed the administration of Papua, and they brought an entirely different mindset to the treatment of the black man, and of course, their women. The White Australia Policy and the treatment of the aborigines by the Australians had caused trepidation for many, including Abel. He had been swept up in the evangelical sentiment of the time and dedicated his life to the protection and empowerment of the Papuan people. Reasons for this concern became evident at this time in numerous cases in the administration of justice by the new regime.

Abel had intervened on many previous occasions on behalf of the Papuans, where it was obvious justice was lopsided or non-existent. This included the 'Gibara incident' in Milne Bay in 1901, in which the Assistant Resident Magistrate Symons and a group of miners went on a punitive expedition shooting locals and burning houses. Abel had a shouting match with Symons' superior, Resident Magistrate Moreton, in the presence of the North Eastern Zone Resident Magistrate Monckton, and the Samarai Hospital Doctor Vaughan, over his lack of action, and threatened to make it public. In Moreton's own words, "I am sorry to say that when Mr. Abel was informed of my intentions, that he became rather immoderate in his talk." Abel took it upon himself to travel south to seek legal advice.

The trial under Chief Judicial Officer, Sir Francis Winter, was a sham and all the accused miners and Symons were let off, while the notorious Steve Wolf, got six months for shooting a woman in the back. "Racial feeling is so general and so strong in this country, that I cannot regard the defendant morally culpable in taking the life of a native.", words declared at the trial by Judge Winter were revealing. They incensed the LMS who wrote to Administrator Le Hunte, resulting in the demotions of Moreton and Symons, and the resignation of Winter.

During this time, Abel was the subject of much vitriol and hate from the resident miners and traders. He had to be accompanied by local bodyguards, and only visited Samarai at night. A contributing factor was his industrial mission approach for practical training of Papuans, and to support the funding of the mission work. This included the running of plantations where the living conditions and pay far outweighed that of the other plantations. This was contrary to the commercial prospects of the colonials.

The imminent transition of the British New Guinea administration to the Australian Federation, the White Australia Policy, and the attitude of the new frontline officers prompted Abel in his visit to Australia in 1902, to speak to Bruce Smith MP of New South Wales, and through him the Attorney General, Alfred Deakin, and the leader of the Labour Party, John Watson. He was after assurances from them that Papua would be developed for the Papuans, and he wanted legislation to support this. He was encouraged by the fact that he was given an audience and the positive tone of these meetings.

When revelations about the Paiwa Massacre in 1903, and the Goaribari Affray in 1904 came to light with the Acting Administrator himself being implicated, Abel felt totally compelled to take action. His letters to the Secretary for External Affairs, Atlee Hunt, and the Minister, William Hughes, and calls for action which caused a sensation in the Brisbane press, led to the establishment of a Royal Commission and the appointment of a more junior officer, Resident Magistrate, Francis Rickton Barton, over Robinson as the Governor. It was too much and led to the unfortunate suicide by Robinson.

The monument erected on the main street of Samarai subsequent to the death of Robinson was inscribed with the epitaph;

"IN MEMORY OF CHRISTOPHER ROBINSON, ABLE GOVERNOR, UPRIGHT JUDGE, AND HONEST MAN, DIED 20TH JUNE 1904, AGED 32 YEARS."

"HIS AIM WAS TO MAKE NEW GUINEA A GOOD COUNTRY FOR WHITE MEN."

Needless to say, Abel was subject to another deluge of condemnation by the white establishment.

We have to judge everybody, including my great grandfather, in the light of the times. Great sacrifices were made by missionaries and members of the civil administration alike, and they faced remarkable challenges. Christopher Robinson was a young man, out of his depth, and elevated too early. It is certainly unfair to ascribe wholesale blame to him. He was in charge of a land habited by generally very warlike tribes and was required to subdue them using the methods of the times, including retributive justice, which he himself believed in, and through subordinates such as Charles Monckton. Peace was required amongst the natives for their own sake, but one suspects that a greater motivation was more often than not, the protection of the invaders, as they went about their business, such as gold mining. Colonial administration and justice seemed to rush to locations, no matter how remote, depending on these activities.

I choose these stories amongst many others to denote the times and exemplify the actions of a man, in Abel, who consistently demonstrated an interest in the welfare of the local people.

It was a sweltering hot Good Friday, 3rd April 1896. The *Olive Branch* was moored some distance off Gabugabuna and Maiwara inside Milne Bay, because of the tide and mudflats. On board were the Reverend Charles William Abel, Mrs. Beatrice Abel, Reverend Frederick William Walker, and his brother Charles Walker.

The *Olive Branch* had been a dramatic improvement from the open whaleboat, *Niue,* from which they had many memories, including the dramatic dash across to Cooktown, in early 1893, when Beatrice was ill and pregnant for the first time.

Mrs. Abel helped her husband on with the jacket over his buttoned up starched shirt. He would suffer the discomfort, as always, of this unsuitable garb in order to best give an impression of his faith. These were people who had, by and large, only seen the worst side of the White Man's ways. Abel was determined to show that he represented a Lord of peace, honour, love, orderliness, and discipline.

In the privacy of his cabin, Beatrice touched his cheek and he kissed her softly. She had not wanted him to visit Maiwara at this stage. Abel had narrowly avoided a nasty altercation there in 1893 when the cult prophet, Tokeriu, was at the height of his powers. Tokeriu and other sorcerers were having their authority challenged by the onslaught of the colonial invaders. The people were being enticed away by the White Man's calico and tobacco, and their religion, which promised a life after death. All things to do with this invader were to be rejected and the people were instructed to kill their pigs, burn their houses, and move into the hills for a great tidal flood was coming and following that an island would arise in Milne Bay covered with goods for the faithful.

Beatrice said, "I release you on this day of the death of our Lord with peace in my heart because you carry His message of salvation through His sacrifice. I pray that the Lord calms my fears and protects you my dearest love."

They had met on the *Brittania* on the way over from England in 1890, and married in Sydney in 1892. It was an enduring love story over forty years that mirrored Abel's love for New Guinea. When apart for even short periods, there would be a letter written every day, and sometimes more than once a day. Beatrice would play a central role in the legendary Kwato Island hospitality, and was her husbands' steadfast reminder of their fundamentalist roots and evangelical mission.

Their first child, also named Beatrice, was born in October 1892, and had been happily playing on board the day before. She was not very well this morning and Beatrice had to remain on board with her.

Abel was five years into his work now and he was gradually replacing all the Loyalty Islands and Polynesian missionaries with Kwato trained teachers, and building up the various mission stations that were established or needed to be established within his London Missionary Society Eastern District. Dealing with long-held cultural beliefs, particularly sorcery, and its grip of fear on the people throughout the Sagarai Valley and down to the coastal villagers, such as Gabugabuna, and Maiwara, was part of the challenge.

Replacing these beliefs, together with the banning of tribal fighting, created a huge void that Abel intended to fill through an industrial mission to prepare the Papuans in a holistic manner for the new era ahead.

Tokeriu had been jailed when his prophecies did not materialize, and this was partially for his own protection from the wrath of the people, who had sacrificed considerably to relocate inland from their coastal villages. There remained elements of resistance though, and hence the concern from Beatrice.

Abel and the two Walker brothers clambered into the rowboat in the familiar routine and settled themselves for the 15-minute pull to the beach. Word of the well-known Reverend from Kwato's visit had preceded him, and unbeknown to the party, there was a reception waiting for them on the walking track into Maiwara. Some of the older warriors had failed in their objective on the last visit. They harboured resentment for the usurping of their established order, and the seemed favouring of their traditional enemies at Wagawaga, across the bay, by the missionaries. They had killed a white miner and wounded another previously. Now they lay in wait in full battle dress to use their spears on the visitors.

On the rowboat, Abel asked the men to bow their heads as he prayed. The sweat ran freely down their backs and dripped off noses as well. The single oarsman, a Logeia man from the *Olive Branch* crew, dipped and pulled.

"Lord, we only seek to do your will. We ask that you open the hearts and minds of these, your children. Guide and protect us on this day, your very day of sacrifice upon the cross.."

The party landed on the grey beach and began the 30-minute walk to Maiwara Village.

"Taubada!!", came the cry from behind them.

It was another member of the crew on a dugout canoe they must have borrowed from a curious local. "Sinebada says you must return immediately. It is the small one."

Abel closed his eyes for a moment. His heart and spirit had been resolved to facing the challenge ahead. His dear friend Fred Walker placed a hand on his shoulder and his thoughts softened as he saw the face of his only child. His eyes opened. "We go back!"

Abel knew before the smaller craft kissed the side of the *Olive Branch*, from the wailing of her mother, that baby Beatrice was dead. It was sudden, inexplicable, and blamed on sunstroke. To this day, the Kwato Church congregation of Maiwara continue to re-enact this event on Foundation Day, of the saving of the life of Abel by the loss of his first child in 1896.

As we trudged down the steps back to the shore from the historical church site on top of Kwato Island one day, Pastor Memari Moutaia of the Kwato Church said to me, "Charles are you going to be a great pastor like your great grandfather?"

As long as I can remember there have been historical books on our house bookshelves with old black and white pictures of stern looking *dimdims* (foreigners) seated in rows, all dressed in button-up, starched clothing. My great grandfather was the serious looking white man with an impressive moustache staring out of the pages of the musty books at home. On later reading, I discovered that he was actually quite a larrikin and practical joker in his time at school and at Cheshunt College. Of course, in the old days you weren't allowed to smile in photographs, or it took so long to take them that the smile had long left your face!

I was ten years old when Pastor Memari Moutaia challenged me. The last thing I wanted at that point was to be a Pastor. Just not cool enough.

We have all come to be where we are from somewhere, somehow. In my family's case, we have a historical colossus in the name of the Reverend Charles William Abel, the famous pioneer of the London Missionary Society, founder of the Kwato Church, and 'champion of the Papuan people'.

My great grandfather is the whole reason we are in Papua New Guinea and Milne Bay today, 131 years later, and there can be no conversation about the essence of who I am without an acknowledgement of the massive legacy, blessing, and burden inherited from this man and an examination of it.

You will have noted that this legacy has also cascaded down into two separate Knights of the Realm from each successive generation, being Sir Cecil Charles Abel, the eldest son of Reverend Abel, and Sir Christopher Charles Abel, the eldest son of Russell William Abel, the second son. Obviously, I am named after my great grandfather and this family legacy is a wonderful blessing. However, it can also be a burden of expectations. I saw how this weighed heavily on my own father. I have tried my best to honour that legacy.

It is also humbling to note, that on my paternal grandmother's side (Ruth Shiela Abel, nee Porteous), we have a great grandfather, Dr. William Porteous who was a pioneer of the Punjab Mission in India (1908–1926), under the Presbyterian Church of New Zealand.

On my mother's side, we are of pure Iokea Village, Gulf Province heritage! I carry the name of my grandfather 'Kauvu' Haro, who was a lay preacher. My granduncle was a powerful sorcerer and I witnessed the power of the incantations from both of them. You will see from later chapters that I have inherited a certain spiritual awareness from both sides of the family.

I daresay, a study of the motivations, intentions, and achievements of Abel are a valuable study in itself, and there are excellent books, such as the three main ones I have drawn from (see References), by my grandfather Russell, David Wetherell, and the thesis by Nancy Lutton, that have purposefully done this. These are more specifically biographical works, unlike mine, and all declare an acknowledgement of his unique and significant personality and achievements. There are criticisms as well, as should be expected in any proper scrutiny.

Abel was a man of great and enduring **faith** and of constantly seeking direct guidance through prayer. He believed in living out this faith, and that a full Christian life necessarily involved **service to others, good works**, and a **moral and disciplined existence.**

He had a lifelong romantic **love and dedication for his wife,** Beatrice. His incessant letter writing to her and all of his children, despite how busy he was, showed a **centrality to the concept of the family unit.**

His love for **physical activity and sport** absolutely shines through from the beginning. You can clearly see how he incorporated it into the daily life of his mission. He took immense pride in the ability of the Kwato cricket team to beat the colonial teams from Samarai, and used sport as a great leveler to build the confidence and pride of the Papuans.

A great **orator**, with plenty of **humour**. He appreciated the artistic abilities of the Massim people in a time when it was unfashionable to do so. He brought a passion for **music** from his own family upbringing, and introduced and taught the Tonic Solfa music system that led to the famous Kwato hym singing.

Ultimately, he was a person that **stood up for the underdog**, as he demonstrated when defending an old Maori woman when living amongst them as a nineteen-year-old boy, or defending an Arab boy in the Port of Said, Egypt, on the return voyage from New Zealand in 1883, and his lifelong defence of the Papuan people.

These are my ***blessings and burdens***, and they speak to me from the pages of history. I hope that they inspire you as well to a life of reward and meaning.

"The major theme in the life of Charles Abel in my view, is his consistent championship of the underdog. His work at Kwato was entirely geared to defending Papuans from predators."
"The missionary surely has plenty to do just teaching, preaching, translation work and pastoral work. None of these things can be shown to have been neglected by Abel. He must therefore be accorded the status of a great man, because of his unusual ability to combine so much extra work into a consistent whole."
(Lutton, Nancy. "Larger Than Life – A Biography of Charles Abel of Kwato", pp 334, 338/339).

James Chalmers, Albert Pearse, Charles Abel, Harry Dauncey, Fred Walker
– South Cape (Suau Island), 1890.

Rev. Charles William Abel, 1863 – 1930.

Beatrice Abel. c 1890.

Chapter 3

Wallaby Country

The group of young warriors squatted around the night fire speaking their language in muted tones. The flickering light revealed lean, muscular bodies, blackened by years of exposure to the sun. The gaping earlobes were weighted with bone ornaments, and the matted hair, sometimes hanging down in a dreadlock pony tail, decorated faces that were grim, and familiar with the killing of men as a way of life.

Around the necks of several of the members were strung the dried fingers of previous victims. These were to be presented to prospective brides before they would even consider the man as a potential husband.

They were fierce Keveri tribesmen. It was November 1935 on the grasslands over the Owen Stanley Range, and five days walk inland from Duram Village on the Abau coast. Duram was half way between Samarai Island and Port Moresby.

A missionary by the name of Cecil Abel of the Kwato Church had arrived the day before with a group of young men and women, talking and behaving in a manner with which they were not familiar. They had never been visited by a missionary before. The only experience they had of the white man was when he came with armed local police and made arrests for murder, and told them how they should live. This white man ate and slept with his local people. He seemed unafraid, despite being without a police escort. It was all very confusing.

In fact, this visiting group was unarmed except for an old Winchester .32, and the spears of some Kunika men with them. They could easily be overcome and killed. Some of the Keveri men had hornbill feathers in their hair and were due for their customary first kill. There was agitation and excitement amongst these warriors as they rubbed shoulders through the night. They decided they would kill their first white man on the wallaby hunt the next day.

The visiting group with Cecil was composed of Phillip, Sila, Bokomani, Davida, Alice (Wedega), Panaeloea – six Kwato stalwarts from Milne Bay, plus five Kwato youth, Ibo and Eremoa – two Kwato trainees from the Fly River, Unan and Mun – two teenage murder convicts from Dimuga (east of Abau), sent to Kwato by Sir Hubert Murray, Frank and four volunteers from Duram, and Maiau, the son of the chief of Amau. Together with Cecil they numbered twenty-two.

They had run short of food at this stage of the Kunika expedition, and it was decided that they would go hunting for wallaby the next morning as this was *magani ena gabu*, **wallaby country.**

It was cold and drizzling the next morning at 4 a.m. when Cecil went around to rouse the men who had volunteered to go on the hunt. The only ones to rise were Maiau, and Frank, one of the carriers. A sense of foreboding and fear had crept into the team at this stage because of the reception of the Keveri which had been rather cold compared to the four previous villages – Dom, Amau, Kuroudi, and Dorevaidi. They were also worn out from the climb up the steep range.

The Keveri warriors could not believe their luck as these three emerged to walk to the hunting ground that morning, that only two men were accompanying the white missionary, and they were Kunika men who had only just met Cecil. They would kill them all at the end of the hunt and return with wallaby and fresh fingers, to then dispose of the rest.

After two hours walking through long kunai grass, the morning sun began to heat up. Without wind it was stifling. Maiau told Cecil in *police motu* that the Keveri had signalled to slow and quiet down.

Within a few moments a large wallaby buck sprang out of the bush and headed adjacent rather than away from the hunters. Cecil raised his rifle to take aim, but it seemed like a blur when Maiau raised his sinew of a throwing arm and felled the animal with his spear from thirty metres away. It was an incredible feat and Cecil caught his breath.

The rest of the day did not result in much luck until the end, when they came upon an unsuspecting group feeding just over the rise ahead. Cecil and the team crept slowly to the ridge line. He carefully took aim at the largest male, and as it looked up, sniffed the air and leapt, the Winchester cracked and it dropped from fifty metres away. The other animals disappeared in an instant and the warriors broke into yells and whoops.

The murder plans changed in that instant. Here was a man unlike any other white man. He travelled unescorted. He ate and slept with the people. He spoke of listening to the Great Spirit, but did not command it. He left his comrades in camp to go with strange warriors, known for their propensity to murder, seemingly without fear. And now he demonstrated that he was a hunter of great skill. How could they possibly kill such a man!

With ancient war chanting resonating the air and the blood of freshly killed *magani* dripping down on ancient grassland they carried the dead wallabies back home, as triumphant hunters.

It was the 4th September 1965 and Christopher Charles Abel and his younger sister Elizabeth (Liz) raced to the Jacksons Airport (now Port Moresby International Airport) to meet their father, who had been medevacked out of Kupiano Airstrip in the Abau District. He had been struck down by sharp pains in his abdomen twenty-four hours earlier at Amau, in the hinterlands of Abau, where there was a thriving mission centre, with a school and a health centre established by the Kwato Church, thirty years earlier. In 1965, Russell William Blair Abel was 60 years old and the Head of the Kwato Church.

Kupiano was the nearest airstrip and Russell was carried by stretcher for a painful sixteen-hour journey through the bush from Amau Mission. He was still alive when loaded onto the aircraft.

Christopher Abel was a 24-year-old, single, fresh faced Agricultural Extension Officer with the Papuan Administration. As the plane landed in Port Moresby and taxied into the bay for such medical events, Christopher thought about all the time his father had been absent in his life throughout his childhood because of the war, boarding school in Australia, and the constant dedication to the work of the Mission.

The medical orderly poked his head out of the aircraft as the steps were lowered, then scrambled down and scampered across the pavement.

"Taubada ia Mase", he shouted over the din of the engines – 'big man is dead'.

There were two calamitous events for the Kwato Church since its inception. These were the death of Reverend Charles William Abel in 1930, and the death of Russell William Abel in 1965.

Mr. Abel went to England in 1930 to talk with the LMS (London Missionary Society). But then, when Mr. Abel was in England, a tragedy happened – he was killed in a road accident. The whole mission felt the loss terribly. Our father and leader had gone from us and no-one was willing to take on what he had been doing. Then Mrs. Abel had to leave us to go to England to look after her husband's affairs. She took Russell and her daughter Badi (Marjorie) with her. We felt more alone than ever, and desperately in need of fresh inspiration and leadership.

So, we went with Cecil and his sister, Phyllis, to a hill station called Duabo, about a day's journey from Kwato. In the peace and quietness of that village among the mountains, Cecil told us about a man he and Russell had met while they were at Cambridge in 1921, an American called **Frank Buchman**. *He had been visiting universities like Cambridge and Oxford telling the students about something important he had realized about living a Christian life. He said that as well as praying to God, people needed to listen to Him every day. When they did this and decided to obey the thoughts they got, miracles happened. Many things happened to the students who tried out this idea. Interest grew so much that, after a while these students were called the Oxford Group. Later on, Dr. Buchman decided on a new name: Moral Re-Armament, and this work became known all over the world.*

The idea of seeking direction from God was a new one to Cecil and Russell, even though they had lived in a Christian home and knew the Bible from their earliest years. But when they got back to

Papua before their father died there was so much to be done that they did not relate this new way of life to the work of the mission.

Now, however, Cecil had been thinking back to what he had heard from Frank Buchman. Up at Duabo he told us that Dr. Buchman had said that, if people faced up to Christ's absolute standards of honesty, purity, unselfishness and love, it was possible for God to speak to them.

Could this be the direction we were all looking for? The guidance of God? We asked ourselves these questions."
(Wedega, Alice, Dame. "Listen My Country", 1981).

"Following what we call the hearo, the 'spiritual revolution' that spread through the Kwato District in late 1931, we found that this new life-changing activity by 1934 could not be contained within the geographic boundaries of the Kwato District."
(Abel, Cecil. "The Kunika Story", undated)

"The story begins in Government House, Port Moresby, in October of 1934, on one hot sweltering afternoon only an hour or two since the sun was directly overhead. In the shade of the verandah the Governor of Papua, Sir Hubert Murray, sat in conference with a tall lean sunburned man who might have been an engineer, or a planter, or an explorer. They were in deep conversation, sipping tea as they spoke. It was a familiar picture. Many writers have drawn such scenes for us. There were coconut mats on the bare boards of the floor, cane chairs, and an impeccable attendant who constantly filled up the cups as they emptied, four and five times. This was a thirsty climate. Below the verandah was a broad undulating lawn. Beyond the lawn was a screen of trees and flowering shrubs - hibiscus, coconut, and bamboo. Beyond the trees was the superb natural harbour of Port Moresby, its huge surface broken by the white square sails of native fishing craft. Finally, on the horizon was the long snow-white line of the barrier reef, pounded forever by the waves. Nearer at hand, just above the trees, the Government jetty prodded out to sea. Some distance from it in the deeper water Sir Hubert's official yacht 'Laurabada' rode sleekly at anchor.

Sir Hubert, the brother of Gilbert Murray the scholar and poet, was a figure not easily forgotten as he sat there at his ease. He had a large spare frame, white hair, close clipped moustache, a white starched tunic buttoning up to the neck, and white duck trousers. Surprisingly, below the white trousers there were enormous black boots. When Sir Hubert left home, he added the further odd touch of a grey trilby and a black umbrella. He could afford to be unconventional. He had been Governor for longer than most people could remember. His just and efficient rule had earned him a unique renown. The Papuans looked upon him as upon a father. His deep affection for the people under his charge was known in colonial administration as the Murray tradition.

Sir Hubert kept to the spirit rather than the letter of the law, and he loved to tell anecdotes to show how well this policy succeeded with the responsive Papuan people. This very morning for the benefit of his guests for lunch he had told the story of Unan and Mun. The presence of the visitor with whom he was now conferring probably recalled the incident to his mind.

Dimuga, the home village of Unan and Mun, was terrorised by a witch, a situation that frequently happened in Papua. This old lady, whether by direct evil influence, by reducing her victims to an extreme state of fear, or by poisoning them, brought about the death of one young man after another. At last, Unan and Mun, the son of the chief, decided that somebody must make a sacrifice if the entire male youth population of the village were not to be wiped out. They waylaid the witch and sent her to the ground with two spears through her. She scarcely made a moan. Unan and Mun then gave themselves up to the village constable fully expecting to serve many years imprisonment for her murder.

Sir Hubert who tried the case knew the strange and horrible power of sorcery. He understood the feelings of the terrified youths of Dimuga and realised that Unan and Mun were knights-errant who had slain a dragon rather than being common murderers. So instead of sending them to prison, he ordered them to attend the technical training centre on Kwato Island of which his visitor was the director. While there, under theoretical detention, Unan and Mun received three years education instead of penal servitude. They proved fully worthy of the experiment and after their three years of detention they stayed on at Kwato, voluntarily.

The other lunch guests eventually departed. The two men who remained got down to their business which was to decide what task Kwato should undertake in the immediate future. The Kwato establishment trained craftsmen, engineers, nurses, and plantation managers with the idea of equipping Papuans to take an increasingly important part in the economic life of their country. However, the purpose was not merely to fill key posts with Papuans. It was to fill these posts with Papuans who were capable of giving the country sound leadership. Therefore, the main stress was laid upon the development of responsibility and sound character. A casual observer might have wrongly thought that technical training in Kwato's spectacular industries and schools was the most important purpose of Kwato.

Sir Hubert often visited Kwato. He was so impressed with the type of Papuan he met there that he wanted to see Kwato's work extended. He wanted what he saw at Kwato for other parts of the country, in particular for areas of where there were disturbing problems. At the time, the worst of these problems was the Dorevaidi headhunting. He wondered if the influence of Kwato could somehow be brought to stop the Dorevaidi from headhunting. The Government had not been able to suppress head hunting. Could these Papuans from Kwato succeed where the Government had failed?

Cecil Abel, Kwato's director, had come to see the Governor in order to discuss Kwato's work. So far in the conversation Sir Hubert had not mentioned the Dorevaidi. It was going to be a daring proposal. He had no idea what Cecil would think of it. At last, he turned to his visitor, and said in his slow, quiet, humorous voice:

"Abel. I have often wished that something might be done about the Dorevaidi. You know the Dorevaidi?"

"By name. I know they are headhunters."

"Exactly"

He looked at Cecil for a moment with a twinkle in his eye.

"Now there's a problem for you"

Cecil nodded, not quite sure how Sir Hubert meant it. Sir Hubert continued.

"They're a wild lot. Each time I go down to Abau I find anything from three to five Dorevaidi up for headhunting, and mark you they don't stop when we get them locked away. This last week in Port Moresby gaol we had one of our best warders murdered with his wife and child their throats slit."

Cecil nodded gravely and sipped his tea. Sir Hubert proceeded again, his voice slightly fanciful as always in spite of the seriousness of his theme.

"We have tried punitive measures. They seem to have no deterrent effect whatsoever. I have given sentences of five and ten years in gaol for murder. There's only capital punishment left. I should be very loath to fall back on that, even if I thought it would be effective."

Both sipped tea. Then Sir Hubert gave what was plainly his weighed judgement on the matter. He said, "Headhunting is a deep-rooted primitive cult. It is part of their whole social structure. I am personally convinced that only something quite new is going to reach the roots of it." Once more there was a twinkle in his eye. Nodding his head sagely but humourously he said, "There's a job Kwato should take on."

Sir Hubert smiled at Cecil as if to say that it was an impossible task, but he wondered about it nevertheless. Then he nodded his head again and added, "Mark you, they're a wild lot. It'll be a long, long job, I warn you."

When Cecil returned from Port Moresby, Sir Hubert's suggestion was discussed at Kwato. Plainly, the first step was to find out more about the Dorevaidi. The name belonged strictly to a small tribe inhabiting a village and some hamlets just north of the main range of the Owen Stanleys. However, it was generally used, as Sir Hubert had used it, to denote a whole group of headhunting tribes allied to them, and inhabiting the district known as the Abau-Kunika. Kunika is the Papuan word for inland districts. The various inland regions are named after the coastal village or town from which the inland regions are approached. The Abau-Kunika was the region behind the coastal village of Abau. This distinction between coastal and inland districts arises because they are inhabited by different races. The coastal people are the more advanced Massims. The inland peoples are the more primitive Melanesians. The headhunters all belong to the primitive inland peoples called Kunikas. The Abau-Kunika region lay some hundred miles east of Port Moresby and reached inland about fifty miles. The chief geographical features included a belt of salt mangrove swamps along the coast. Behind that there was a coastal plain some miles wide overgrown with dense tropical jungle. Behind that again there was the main range of the Owen Stanleys with peaks up to the 11 000 feet high Mount Clarence.

The people at Kwato discovered a good deal about the Dorevaidi from Government records. From their beginning, these records told of headhunting and warfare among the Dorevaidi tribes. It was hard to believe that any human beings could be such ruthless killers. The Dorevaidi people would slaughter any unarmed man they came across as casually as a farmer shoots a rabbit. However, most of their killings were not casual. They stalked and waylaid victims according to well-laid plans. They made armed raids on neighbouring villages. They did not actually cut off the hand of their victims but a little finger which was a convenient trophy to carry around. They killed mainly because they enjoyed killing, but added spurs were often revenge or matrimony. Before giving their hand in marriage most Dorevaidi maidens required a little finger cut from some wretch killed in her honour. Some girls demanded a whole string of little fingers.

The happy hunting ground for fingers was the coast where the less warlike Massims lived. It was safer to headhunt, or more exactly, finger-hunt along the coast. Life for the unfortunate coastal peoples was therefore dominated by fear of the mountaineers. The coastal peoples would gaze in terror at the Owen Stanley peaks. Up there were the eyries of the Dorevaidi.

Some weeks after Murray's conference with Cecil Abel, a government officer named Humphreys visited Kwato. He had once served as Resident Magistrate in the Dorevaidi region. Therefore, he did not escape a bombardment of questions. Not that he would have wished to escape for he loved talking of his Dorevaidi days. After supper, he sat on the dark verandah with a number of the Kwato staff. He said that the authorities had failed either to cudgel or cajole the Dorevaidi into peaceful habits. The women were even tougher than the men. The women were the real inspiration of the cult of killing.

Humphreys told the story of his last trip inland. This was a tale of hide-and-seek with murderers through the jungles and over the ranges. It ended in Dorevaidi villages with the killers handcuffed. Humphreys held court and harangued a sullen mob on the benefits of peace.

Before setting off for the coast with his retinue of policemen, culprits, and witnesses he sat down for a quick meal. While he was eating some women grouped themselves at a respectful distance. Swaying and swinging their grass petticoats the women intoned for him a little dirge. He was greatly heartened by this unexpected gesture. He smiled graciously in acknowledgement before he marched off with his company.

His police sergeant said in agitated tones, "Taubada, the song of the women was not good."

"Not good?"

"...the words..."

The police sergeant proceeded to inform Humphreys that the picturesque farewell had been addressed not to Humphreys but to the prisoners. Bound as the prisoners were for long terms in gaol the prisoners doubtlessly needed every aid to morale. The women had chanted, "We will be faithful to you because you are killers. We will only give our favours to real men."

Humphreys concluded, "So I gave my official blessing to Dorevaidi anarchy".

Nevertheless, there was ample evidence in all that Humphreys had said to show that he had grown to respect his awkward charges. In spite of everything, he had become fond of them. He strongly supported Sir Hubert's proposal that people from Kwato should go into their country, and his enthusiasm tipped the scale. After Humphreys visit, there was never any serious doubt that people from Kwato would do it.

(Abel, Russell and Mackay, Dermot. "They Broke Their Spears", undated).

The subsequent mission work in the Amau-Kunika area was remarkable to say the least. Killings and tribal warfare ceased totally for at least twelve years, until a single case of homicide occurred. The people of Dou, Domara, Kuroudi, Dorevaidi, and parts of Keveri relocated to the central location of Amau with the generosity of Chief Belei (father of Maiau of the first expedition with Cecil). A mission centre was built there, and health and education services were imparted until the Second World War arrived in 1942. The work continued after the War until Russell's death in 1965.

The other chiefs of note were Ofekule of the Dorevaidi, Sibodu of the Kuroudi, Biruma of the Dou, and Rabu of Nebula.

Russell Abel was my paternal grandfather who, judging by the hundreds who attended his funeral on Kwato Island in 1965, made quite an impression of his own. I'm told by Dad that he was a gentle man, full of humour and "loved by all". I've seen brilliant artistic cartoons that he penned in loving letters to my Dad, his first-born son. Grandma Sheila, with whom we spent much time, wore her wedding band to the end, and I recall her saying on several occasions that she was looking forward to being reunited with her husband.

The work of a missionary meant that there were long absences by Russell from the family, and my distinct impression is that these absences and a reluctance to physical expressions of affection, despite the obvious love he felt for his family, were felt by my father. As a result, he had difficulty in later years expressing public affection for his wife and children.

In comparing my two grandfathers, I would say that Russell was a quieter, artistic man, very stable, and totally dedicated to his task. His student-day letters are long and descriptive, but very entertaining and full of fun. He was able to run the Mission successfully, without controversy, for thirteen years, from 1952 to 1965, until his death at the age of sixty. He was sufficiently of focused mind to write a comprehensive biography of his famous father, as commissioned by the New Guinea Evangelical Society in 1934.

Russell, with the help of Benoma Dagoela, completed the translation of the New Testament into the Suau language, which was a work started by Fred Walker in 1890, and both their fathers, (Benomas father was Dagoela Manurewa[1], son of the head man of Savaia Village).

This was a significant work as only the Gospel of Mark had been published at that point. The *Riba Harihariuna* also represents the defining authority today of classic Suau, as explained by my father in *Ta Alina Suau* (the Suau Dictionary). Russell Abel held a Master of Arts degree in anthropology from Cambridge University.

Cecil was the elder of the two and exuded many of the charismatic and oratory attributes of his father. He had an amazing memory all the way up to his death on the 25th of June 1994 at the age of 91. From the moment he began to play any role in the Mission work he began to estrange from the major financial sponsors at the time by adopting more modernist theological language and associations. They ended up severing ties with the Kwato Mission. Cecil had to relinquish the position as head of the Mission in 1951, after running the mission from 1931, following the death of his father. He played a part in the Second World War, supporting the Allies with his local knowledge of Milne Bay and the Northern Province. Russell was not able to

---

[1] *There are three versions of this surname, two from the writings of Wetherell – Manuwera, Manuegu, and the version used here from Lutton – Manurewa.*

pass the age and medical requirements for enlistment and spent this time in Sydney on work gangs preparing for an invasion.

Cecil was not particularly successful in business, but then began a career in politics which suited him more and he made a substantial contribution to the early movements towards independence and the necessary preparations for nationhood that are not fully appreciated. This is apart from a Knighthood in 1982 sponsored by his former student, and long-time friend, the Grand Chief Sir Michael Somare, whom he lectured in political science at the new Administration College. He held a Bachelor of Arts degree in anthropology from Cambridge University.

Russell died of strangulated hernia on board a medivac flight out of Amau in the hinterlands of Abau District on the 4th of September 1965. This was three years before my arrival on earth so I did not have the opportunity to meet him. This was also the case with my father and his grandfather, the Reverend Charles William Abel, who survived forty years of frontier life in Papua, only to be killed by a London speeding car in 1930, eleven years before Dad arrived. The outcome was a more prominent role by Sir Cecil in all our lives, but more particularly, Dad, who revered his uncle.

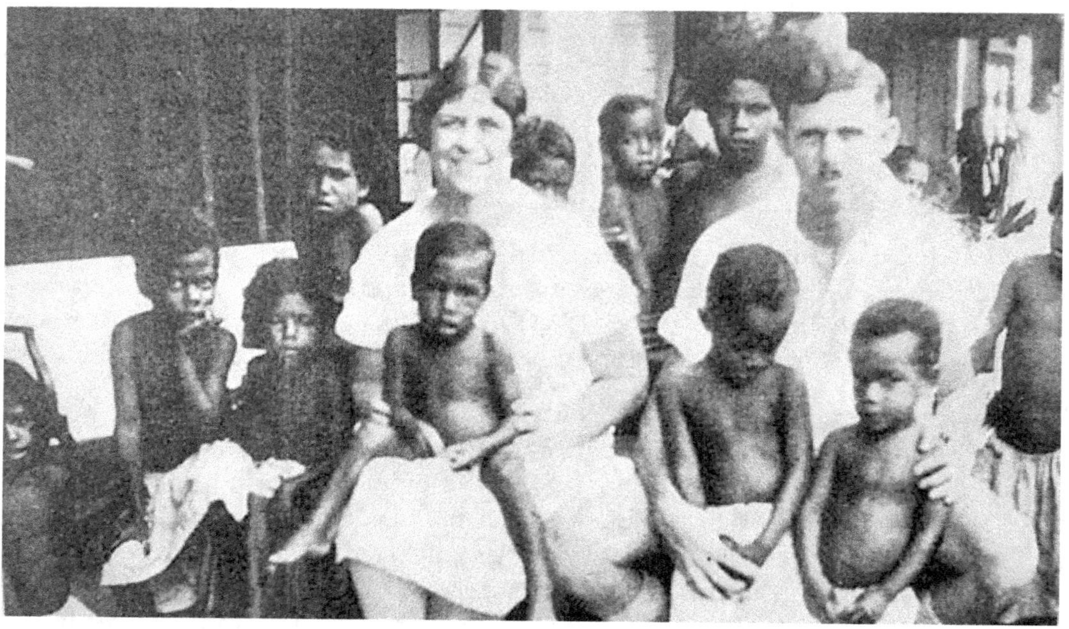

Phyllis Abel and Cecil Abel, with Kwato children – 1931.

Russell Abel and Sheila Abel, c. 1960.

Sir John Hubert Murray 1861 – 1940,
Lieutenant Governor of Papua 1908 – 1940.

Abau-Kunika tribesmen - Biruma 2nd from left, Maiau far right, next to his father, Chief Belei. c. 1930.

Chapter 4

Monster on the Horizon

It was the afternoon of the 25th of August 1942. Aboard the *Osiri*, Cecil Abel and his skipper, Sila, and crew were tense and frustrated. They were at the Giligili Jetty in Milne Bay, in Australian New Guinea.

It was the eve of the Battle of Milne Bay and the Japanese war machine was coming, a terrifying, undefeated ***monster on the horizon***, devouring everything in its path.

The small harbour at Giligili was the seaside service point for the Milne Force headquarters at Hagita, as well as for the only operational airstrip, *No.1 Strip,* or *Gurney Field*, named after the late RAAF squadron leader, Charles Gurney.

Cecil, who had been the head of the Kwato Mission since 1931, volunteered himself and crew with the launch, *Osiri,* to provide logistical support to the Allied forces. He writes of the mood at the time;

"..they (previous writers) fail to convey the all-pervading sense of fear and inevitable defeat in the face of a ruthless, invincible foe."

"..the feeling, almost of despair , that prevailed everywhere. You had to know what this was like in order to assess its effect on men, and especially on our leader's capacity to react with cool heads and to make reasonable judgements and decisions." **(Abel, Cecil. "The Battle of Milne Bay — Six Key Factors that Helped to Snatch Victory From Defeat", 1992)**

There were so many rumours going around regarding the impending Japanese attack. Confirmation had been received of a naval assault heading from Rabaul as well as a separate dispatch from Buna on the north coast, but weather had hampered aerial surveillance and possible counter attacks. Were they coming over the mountains from Taupota, or landing on the north or south coast of the bay? Perhaps all three?

The incidences of Japanese surveillance planes and Zero attacks had intensified, keeping the 75th and 76th Royal Australian Air Force (RAAF) squadrons of P40 Kittyhawks busy flying out of the recently completed airstrip.

Major General Cyril Clowes had just taken up command and was unsure whether to extend his forces to meet the enemy, or keep them congregated to protect the primary asset of the airstrip. The Japanese were after the airfields from where they would strike at Port Moresby and then Australia. The Allies had the intention to bolster the defences of Eastern Papua and then attack Rabaul, which was the main Japanese base.

Clowes had been sent to replace the command of Brigadier John Field, who had done a marvelous job of construction of the three airstrips with United States army engineers and 1 200 local labourers. Field had also managed to keep his activities relatively secret from the enemy, which proved to be vital. Clowes and his young subordinates were not going to admit to these successes though, as they were there to 'clean up' the situation.

As usual, the Americans, being predominantly of the 46th Engineers Battalion, and making up ten percent of the Milne Force, were difficult to command, and seemed to want their orders direct from General Douglas MacArthur himself.

Malaria was wreaking havoc by infecting at least 250 troops each day, rendering them effectively useless. And the weather was unbelievable. The militia men of the 7th Brigade had only served within Australia and had never seen rain and mud like this. This was the wet season in one of the wettest places on earth.

Clowes' job was to protect the airfield at all costs and destroy the enemy. Yet, this was an army that had never been defeated.

Thankfully, the more experienced 18th Brigade under Brigadier George Wootten had also arrived on the 12th of August. This brought the Milne Force strength to close to ten thousand men including 600 RAAF airmen.

Australian control of the protectorate of Papua, consisting of the southern and eastern portions of the island, was gained from the British in 1906. Later, at the Paris Peace Conference in 1920, Australian Prime Minister, William Hughes, lobbied for a mandate over the territory of New Guinea, which comprised the remainder of the island in addition to the Bismarck Archipelago.

The native population was estimated at 1.8 million, mostly tribal and clan based, with a diverse range of languages and cultures. The European population was 6 000 and consisted largely of government officials, copra and rubber planters, gold miners, and missionaries. The largest settlements with European populations were Rabaul, Samarai Island, and Port Moresby.

For the purposes of the Australian Army's administration, the two territories were collectively designated the 8th Military District, commanded by Major General Basil Morris. The soldiers under his command principally fell into three groups. The first was the 30th Brigade of which, at that time, only the 49th Battalion was in Port Moresby. The second was the Papuan Infantry Battalion, raised in 1940 for the defence of Papua and comprising Papuans led by European officers and non-commissioned officers (NCOs). The final group was the New Guinea Volunteer Rifles, formed by Europeans living in New Guinea who were determined to play a role in the defence of their homes.

Morris had to contend with numerous problems. There were insufficient naval and air assets to adequately defend Port Moresby and the soldiers garrisoning the town were poorly trained. Tensions in New Guinea climaxed in 1942. By 3 February the Japanese were bombing Port Moresby provoking mass panic, while the civil administration began to unravel. Martial law was declared and Morris assumed absolute power in New Guinea from the island's Administrator.

On 21 February, the Australian New Guinea Administrative Unit (ANGAU) was formed to supervise labour, maintain law and order, and to oversee native welfare. Even with this development, the situation in New Guinea continued to deteriorate, prompting stricter measures. On 10 June, the territories of Papua and New Guinea were amalgamated to form one territory called Australian New Guinea. **(Anderson, Nicholas. "The Battle of Milne Bay, 1942", 2018)**

By mid-1942, the Japanese empire was at its peak and was still yet to face defeat on the battlefield. They had established a significant base at Rabaul, and by late August had commenced the Kokoda campaign to reach Port Moresby on the south coast, from Buna on the north coast of New Guinea, and planned to attack a newly sighted airfield and base at Milne Bay. The Battle of the Coral Sea had been inconclusive and the Japanese Imperial Navy had failed in its objective to take Port Moresby by sea.

The Japanese had rolled irrepressibly down through the Malaysian Peninsula, wreaking death and destruction. The traditional colonial masters had been rather pathetic protectors in the first instance, despite their assurances. Notwithstanding the Chinese and South-East Asian experiences with Japanese aggression, it was still a horrific and shocking realization.

Their resentment of the historic treatment by the Western powers, cultural overtones of racial superiority, the Bushido warrior code, and religious loyalty to the emperor, translated into an unstoppable, manic fighting machine. Unfortunately, this machine brought out some of the worst examples of human cruelty in a systemic manner yet seen. The Rape of Nanking in China had been a prelude of this.

There were five small 'local' boats held at Giligili under orders including the *Osiri*. The others were – *Royal Endeavour, Bronzewing, Elevala and Gitana.* They were out of fuel and food and requested to travel the thirteen kilometres east to Ahioma, where the ANGAU depot was. This was refused on the 24th of August.

On the 25th, there was increasing concern about the pending attack, and Lieutenant Colonel Meldrum, who was the CO of the 61st Battalion, was worried about his Company which had gone to Ahioma, and their 17 Platoon which had patrolled all the way to East Cape. He ordered the return of them all to Giligili and instructed the boats to move to Ahioma and assist in the repatriation. 2IC, Major Harry Wiles, was sent to Ahioma to oversee the orders.

At this point in Cecil's words, "We cast off and moved away from the Giligili Jetty. Sila, the skipper of the *Osiri* knew of the urgency of our store's predicament. As a matter of routine however, he came down from the bridge or the helmsman's cabin and asked, "Where to Taubada?" It was then it happened. As clearly as if someone had been standing behind me, something, someone said quite simply, "Spend the night at Wagawaga." (That was Wagawaga on the south or opposite side of the bay). I repeated what I heard and told Sila, "We'll spend the night at Wagawaga". Sila looked at me hard and repeated, "Wagawaga?" "Yes" I said, "Wagawaga. And we'll go over for our stores tomorrow morning."[1]

That evening Special Naval Landing Force units *Kure No.5* and *Sasebo No.5* of the Rabi (Rabe) Operation, on two troop ships and escorted by seven warships rounded East Cape in heavy rain and approached a mist shrouded base of Milne Bay. On board was a force of 1 200 men of the Imperial Japanese Navy. Their local guide, from Buna in Oro Province, who had worked in the area previously, strained his eyes to make out familiar landmarks. It wasn't long before he was sure he could see the extruding point at Rabe chosen as the site to disembark and best take the airstrip. He was gravely mistaken. It was actually Wahuhuba, a point closer to Ahioma, thirteen kilometres to the east of the intended site. This played a major bearing on the outcome of the Battle of Milne Bay.

Further north several hundred men of the *Tsukioka Unit* had left the Japanese base at Buna on the 24th for Taupota. They only made it as far as Goodenough Island where they were attacked from the air and scuttled. Obviously, this also had a major bearing on the troops subsequently available to the landing force.

Reinforcements of 700 additional troops, together with Commander Yano Minoru, and supplies from Rabaul, did manage to land four days after the initial landing though. This brought the total number of Japanese to 1 943.

Meanwhile, of the five small boats at Giligili, the *Gitana* had failed to depart because of an absconded crew, the *Osiri* headed to Wagawaga and the *Bronzewing, Elevala* and *Royal Endeavour* arrived at Ahioma at 8:30 p.m. and were then advised to load any of the sickest soldiers, resupply and return to Giligili. The others with 2IC Wiles would walk back. With loading completed the boats departed at midnight.[2]

The Japanese had decided on their disembarkation point and turned in towards the shore. As fate would have it, they collided directly with the three smaller allied vessels leaving from Ahioma. The barges' spotlights picked them out immediately and a massacre ensued.

---

[1] *There is a slight divergence between the account given by Nicholas Anderson in The Battle of Milne Bay 1942, and the written account of Cecil Abel, as to the reasons for the departure from Giligili. Cecil does not mention the evacuation orders which is interesting as he and the vessel, Osiri, conducted numerous such rescue missions following the attack by the Japanese. One such account is given below.*

[2] *Nicholas Anderson only mentions three boats being instructed – 'Bronzewing', 'Elevala' and 'Dadosee'. Perhaps Osiri, Royal Endeavor and Gitana received separate orders. Cecil mentions five boats being available at Giligili. He does not mention a Dadosee. Perhaps Dadosee and Royal Endeavor were the same boat?*

Most of the casualties were the result of machine gun fire across the decks and at the men in the water.

Three of the Australians were taken alive and subject to the infamous Japanese interrogation. They were never seen again.

Cecil and the crew of the *Osiri* watched the fireworks from Wagawaga on the other side of the bay, as the escort Japanese war ships bombarded KB Mission thinking it was the allied headquarters at Giligili. Again, this was an error based on the earlier navigation error. It was clear the invasion had begun.

One interesting point that was overlooked in historical accounts was the ability of the Japanese warships to disappear during the day and re-emerge at night to continue shelling the Allied positions. Aerial searches were in vain. Cecil explained that the ships would retreat in the darkness before dawn across to Sewa Bay at Normanby Island and cover themselves with camouflage netting. He said it was a testament to their local knowledge. The fatal initial landing mistake was caused by bad weather.

The following morning as the *Osiri* made her way back to Giligili to receive the bad news, the Kittyhawks launched into the clouds in sprays of mud off the marston matting clad Gurney Field and roared over the beached Japanese, releasing 1 500 rounds from their machine guns with each pass. These planes had nearly left the day before out of concern that a possible bombardment in the pending invasion would incapacitate the airfield. Clowes did not let them go.

The Japanese landing error and subsequent delayed attack on the landing strips and Allied Headquarters enabled a daily aerial strafing of the exposed Japanese. The Kittyhawk's were unhindered as the Japanese air force were preoccupied at Guadalcanal and Kokoda. Lack of proper surveillance had also led them to underestimate the forces at Milne Bay.

This had a significant impact on the Japanese ability to operate at daytime so a lot of movement and fighting took place at night. This added to the delay on the Japanese assault on the intended target. It was difficult enough with the rain and muddy conditions. As the Japanese were repulsed later on, many of the dead were found with swollen and rotting feet. Added to all this was the high incidence of malaria.

What followed over the next two weeks was a war of attrition from Wahuhuba (Ahioma) to *No.3 Strip* at Kainako, just beyond Rabe (Rabi), and back.

Also on 30 August, Captain Bicks led another patrol, including the ever-reliable Lieutenant Robinson, as far forward as Motieau Creek and K.B. Mission. Bicks' patrol did not encounter any significant resistance, but the men were appalled to discover examples of the enemy's barbarity. First, passing the Gama River, Bicks found a row of neatly laid out Japanese bodies. Every man was naked, with bandages covering wounds of the head and limbs. In each case, a bullet wound marked the individual's heart; it appeared the Japanese had killed their own wounded.

Continuing towards K.B. Mission, there were more shocking discoveries. A dead Papuan was spotted, his hands tied behind his back with signal wire, with bullet wounds and bayonet punctures marking his body. More chilling was the discovery of two dead soldiers from Bicks' own 61st Battalion. These men had been shot and bayoneted after being taken prisoner, their bodies then mutilated and their faces disfigured beyond recognition. This evidence of Japanese cruelty stoked bitter feelings of resentment.

Warrant Officer Robert Crawford recalled, 'It was only when we got to Milne Bay that we found first hand [evidence of the Japanese brutality] ... They were killing people straight away from the word go. Even the army chaps, they overran them, they were bayoneted and shot to death straight away ... I don't think any Australian prisoners were taken at all and they lost lots of good, wonderful young men. So that was when the hatred ... started and never diminished from then on.' **(Anderson, Nicholas. "The Battle of Milne Bay 1942", 2018).**

The climax was on the night of the 30th of August when the exhausted Japanese made suicidal charges across the open space of the incomplete *No.3 Strip* (This was the first airstrip of the three, when approaching from the east. The operational airstrip, *No.1 Strip*, at Giligili, was between *No.3 Strip*, and *No.2 Strip*, which was at Waigani, further west.).

The Allied troops were waiting with trained machine guns and some 300 Japanese were essentially slaughtered. There stands at Kainako, today, a memorial marker to the dead on both sides and marking the end of the Japanese war advance. A separate memorial to the Japanese was established for the 80th anniversary of the battle at Kalo, adjacent to Wahuhuba.

The premonition had saved Cecil's life and the *Osiri* was the only remaining operational support vessel. His intricate local knowledge, ability to speak Suau, and trip after trip delivering supplies and loading wounded from that time contributed to the first land-based defeat of the Japanese up to that point. It was a major psychological victory and turning point in the war.

On the 4th of September 1942 the Japanese troops were being driven back towards their original landing point in a reciprocation of the bloody creek-by-creek battle a few days earlier. It was at the crossing of the Goilanai River, just past the location of the current township of Alotau. Here, a 28 year-old hairdresser from Crows Nest, in Queensland was to distinguish himself in battle. There were many heroes in the Battle of Milne Bay on both sides. In this case though, Corporal John French of the 2/9th Infantry Battalion of the 18th Brigade, decided to single handedly take on three machine gun nests.

The Australians had taken heavy casualties that morning after crossing the river under withering fire. Attempts to flank the enemy by going inland had failed and the direct approach was the last option. They were now pinned on the eastern bank under fire from three machine guns.

French, in his quiet way, told the men of his section to lay low while he went forward alone to avoid further casualties. The men's minds were seared with the death all around them, and particularly of their mates. They had seen first-hand the senseless cruelty of the Japanese and their determination it seemed to die in the cause for their country. Yet, they had pressed on, pushing the enemy to this point. The fortitude of such young men in the face of violent death, and fearsome opposition, is incredible to say the least.

Corporal French went forward alone, against three machine guns, no less. He was able to silence the first one with grenades. Had a good cricketing arm perhaps. He then returned for more grenades before attacking and silencing the second nest. He then proceeded to take on the third nest shooting his Tommy Gun from the hip. He was shot in the chest, but battled on and died while taking out the last nest.

French was posthumously awarded the Victoria Cross, which is the highest award for gallantry in the face of the enemy that can be awarded to British and Commonwealth forces. (There were nine recipients of the Victoria Cross from actions in the Second World War in the Territories of Papua, and New Guinea. The other eight were – Newton (Salamaua), Chowne (Dagua), Derrick (Finschafen), Kelliher (Lae), Kenna (Wewak), Kingsbury (Isurava), Partridge (Bouganville), Sukanaivalu (Bouganville).)

In August 1992, Sir Cecil Abel stood at the memorial of Corporal John French, on the banks of the Goilanai River, and spoke on the commemoration of the 50th Anniversary of The Battle of Milne Bay. He said later;

"I was on the *Osiri* at KB the afternoon Corporal French was killed. When I spoke at this Service, I told how we had been asked by Col. Arnold, at KB, to try and take out a soldier who had been shot in the stomach, at this very spot (where the service was being held). Although it was late in the afternoon, we were able to get in and out without being spotted by enemy mortar positions. We got this wounded man safely back to the Giligili Field Dressing Station and he was later evacuated on the hospital ship *Manunda*. That was 50 years ago and I had never heard whether he survived."

"At the end of this memorial service and before we had dispersed, one of the Australian ex-servicemen stood up and said;

"Excuse me, but I was that man you came to rescue! If you had not come for me that afternoon, I would have died that night."'

"We were all greatly moved and overcome by what Harry Triffit told us. That was his name. He now lives in Tasmania and has 29 grandchildren! I had never told that story before, and if I had not told it then, he would never have known how he came to be taken out to safety before it was too late."

In all, close to 2 000 Japanese fought in the Battle of Milne Bay. 625 were killed and 311 wounded. Almost 9 000 Allied troops took part, of which 90 percent were Australian. 181 were killed, and 206 wounded. This pales in comparison to other major battles of the Second World War, but its significance lies in that it was the first land-based victory against the fearsome Japanese army in the Pacific, and marked a turning of the tide in the war.

The 80th Anniversary of the Battle of Milne Bay was celebrated on the 27th of August 2022, with a fly over by two F15 Jets of the RAAF. The Chairman of the Organizing Committee was a Mr. Jeffrey Abel, my youngest brother.

Cecil Abel was also credited for recommending and constructing 'Abel's Field' airstrip at Gasari, one of three airstrips he helped to build in the mountains on the Oro and Milne Bay Provincial borders, using local labor and under instructions from the US Army. The first C-47 Dakota transport plane landed there on the 19th October 1942. The field was used to airlift troops and supplies to support the allied advance to Buna, Gona, and Sanananda on the north coast.

Cecil was only acknowledged later in his life for his contributions to the war effort with a pension from the Australian Government, following much effort from his son Andrew Abel.

Sir Cecil Abel and Harry Triffit – at the 50th anniversary commemorations of the Battle of Milne Bay, 1992.

The Osiri at Kwato; The vessel used by Cecil Abel to transport supplies and the wounded in the Second World War.

Corporal John French, 1914 – 1942, recipient of the Victoria Cross in the Battle of Milne Bay.

Squadron Leader Keith "Bluey" Truscott, Commanding Officer of No. 76 Squadron RAAF, taxiing along Marston Matting at Milne Bay in September 1942.

Chapter 5

We The People

"Sir Cecil loved this country very much, and his vision was to see the country and the people freed from the yoke of colonialism. He was a man of very high principles and impregnable Christian virtues."

"He was humble, loved his family, and was the epitome of kindness. Sir Cecil was one of my dearest friends, mentor, and confidante, who was a scholar, soldier, and statesman."

(Sir Michael Thomas Somare, Post-Courier, Monday 4th July 1994, – extracts from eulogy)

My memories of visiting Sir Cecil's Waigani home with my father have certain highlights that are so clear. I've already described some of them in the charismatic, energetic, wonderful storyteller that he was. Dad adored him, and my brother Owen and I were always totally enthralled as young lads. He was in his twilight years but you could also see signs of his compulsiveness and disorganization in the ramshackle house and scattered papers.

Certainly, a highlight was the very obvious affection between the Grand Chief, Sir Michael Somare, and Sir Cecil. I witnessed it on several occasions between them at the Waigani house with the tea and biscuits flowing from the wonderful Lady Semi Abel. The familiarity, camaraderie, easy jokes, and shared history was obvious. It was like watching two brothers enjoying each other's company. On one occasion, Sir John Guise was there as well, and some of the jokes and loud laughter would make you blush. What a treat.

Even when Sir Michael was not there, Sir Cecil always referred to him as "The Chief". Such was the respect.

With a father such as Reverend Charles William Abel there is no doubt that Cecil, Russell, and their siblings had very clear impressions from the outset on the meaning of life and which way was up. Their mother, Beatrice played no small part in this and you do get the impression of somewhat overbearing parents but always with an absolutely loving intent.

Even when it came to politics, there was exposure from the very early days;

"In 1909 my father was on a long leave in England. He rented a small detached house for the family in Streatham. We were there when Lloyd George's famous budget was thrown out of the House of Lords and this was followed by the General Elections that brought the Liberals into power. As a boy

of five or six I joined my father and his brother in campaigning for Warren, the Liberal candidate for that electorate. I remember walking around Wandsworth Common with a large placard of Warrens picture in front of me and being pelted and jeered at by the little snobs in Eton collars who were supporting Kimber, the Conservative candidate. Abel's political convictions were part of his life and for us, his children this meant the sort of breakfast table discussion that involved us all and impressed us all deeply.

The Abel's were Congregationalists and jealous of their right to choose their own minister and run their Chapels without interference from any other body. I doubt if any religious body was as autonomous or as democratic as the Congregationalists were a hundred years ago. This outlook was also reflected in political allegiances. Abel and his whole family, especially his brother, were active Liberals. At the time of Campbell -Bannerman, Asquith and Lloyd George, being a Liberal corresponded to what we would now call a radical or even a socialist. And they took their politics seriously." **(Cecil Abel, "The Impact of Charles Abel", 2nd Waigani Seminar UPNG, 31/05/1968).**

Charles was a remarkable combination of a liberal, free thinker, and yet traditionalist at the same time. He was a fundamentalist in terms of his foundation beliefs in the literal interpretation of the Bible, yet came up against so many obstacles because of his desire to go beyond the normal missionary template of the times and translate Christianity into a more holistic solution. Like Livingstone in Africa, and Booker T Washington in the deep south of slave country in the US, he wanted to present a spiritual and moral prescription, but also **the practical means for a new people, a new nation to take charge of its own affairs**.

"Charles was looking ahead 50 years, 60 years, and even 80 years ahead to the time when Papuans would have to take responsibility for their whole country. That is why he stressed the importance of training young men and women in new skills and industries that no Papuans had ever done before. The Abels and those Papuans working with them were laying the foundations for building a new nation. This would mean self-reliance, discipline, hard work and a new sense of responsibility and caring for others. There were many failures and disappointments, but Papuans were learning to do these things for themselves and to draw their strength direct from God. People could see the new standard in many small ways. Kwato people did not chew betelnut. They spoke better English than anywhere else in Papua." **(Cecil Abel, "The Kwato Way", 1987).**

Kwato was the literal manifestation of this, and many of the *isi mulita* (2nd generation) and subsequent generations of Kwato-trained Papuans filled the ranks of the new political and public service hierarchy. There were accusations of elitism, but Charles took the only practical course he felt was available to him to begin to meaningfully prepare a cohort, given what he perceived as the imminent existential threat to the natives of British Papua at the time.

Cecil and Russell were both born at Kwato and seemed to have little choice in their destiny to carry the mantle forward, and they certainly seemed to adopt this wholeheartedly. I have mentioned earlier that this presumption of inheritance was a fundamental breach in more ways than one, that perhaps manifested down the road. But the point here being that there was a clear frame of mind from the genesis of **service to a cause**.

When Cecil was asked by the Administrator, Sir Hubert Murray, to take on the position of Lecturer in Political Science in 1963 at the newly established Administration College (ADCOL), it was fortuitous. He was always a natural politician, communicator, and teacher. Armed with his Cambridge University degree in Arts, with a major in Anthropology, his twenty-one years running an industrial mission, his pro-Papuan, liberal ideas, together with the culmination of international anticolonial sentiment, and a sympathetic Australian administration for a timely transition to self-government and even independence, it was an opportune chance to redeem himself. He even came with a Milne Bay wife, Semi Bwagagaia, whom he married in 1951, a time when such interracial unions were certainly frowned upon.

The Port Moresby Teacher's College, The Papuan Medical College and ADCOL were the pre-eminent tertiary institutions that emerged at this time. ADCOL was established to provide additional tertiary training to indigenous public servants, starting in August 1963.

Some of the students who attended ADCOL included, Michael Somare, Albert Maori Kiki, Oala Oala-Rarua, Gavera Rea, Joseph Nombri, Sinaka Goava, Jack Karakuru, Cromwell Burau, and Bill Warren.

Somare had been trained as a teacher at Sogeri in 1956, returned to Sogeri in 1962, after some teaching work, to do the Queensland Junior Certificate, then worked as a radio announcer in Wewak before coming to ADCOL in 1965 aged 29.

They formed the basis of what came to be known as the **'Bully Beef Club'**, together with such people as Reuben Taureka from the Papuan Medical College, Ebia Olewale from the Port Moresby Teachers College, and inaugural 1964 House of Assembly members, John Guise, Paul Lapun, Pita Lus, Barry Holloway, and Tony Voutas.

Cecil Abel was a foundation member of the 'Bully Beef Club', and as their lecturer at ADCOL, played a major role in guiding and mentoring the energetic young leaders. You can just imagine some of the classroom interactions in 1964 and 1965.

In May 1965, the House of Assembly established the Select Committee on Constitutional Development. It was Chaired by John Guise, with members, Nicholas Brokam, Sinake Giregire, Pita Simogen, Paul Lapun, Tei Abal, Wegra Kenu, Dirona Abe, and John Gunther. L.W Johnson, and Wally Watkins were appointed (official) members.

In January and March of 1967, two submissions to the Select Committee were signed by 13 men – Reuben Taureka, Gerai Asiba, Penuelli Anakapu, Oala Oala- Rarua,

Michael Somare, Ebia Olewale, Maori Kiki, Joseph Nombri, Ilimo Batton, Elliot Elijah, Sinaka Goava, Kamona Walo, and Cecil Abel.

Cecil was the only non-indigenous member of '**the thirteen angry men**', agitating for a speedier movement to self-government for the Australian Territory.

On the 13th of June 1967 the establishment of the **Papua New Guinea Union Party – PANGU** was announced. Its initial members were the 'angry 13' and nine members from the House of Assembly. Its clear intentions were the replacement of the Australian Administration with self-rule and then independence.

Coincidentally, thirteen Pangu affiliated members were elected to the 1968 House of Assembly and Cecil was one of them as the Member for Milne Bay (Regional). Later that year, he drafted the party's economic policy, which emphasised the need to increase overseas capital investment, raise exports in both primary and secondary sectors, reduce imports and encourage import replacement, greatly increase secondary industry, and move from a subsistence to a cash economy. The policy stated that: **"We must aim for a reasonable equality of wealth between black and white, or rather, between haves and have nots."**

There was still a general uncertainty in the populace and certainly in the Highlands and amongst the expatriate commercial establishment and elements of the administration to the prospect of early self-government, and PANGU was relegated to the Opposition and suffered a degree of hostility in those early days.

By the 1972 Elections it was much more clearly a referendum on the future of the status of the territory. PANGU maintained its hard-line push for immediate self-government and the United Party, led by Tei Abal, held the more conservative, go slow, economic risk averse, anti-independence view. They prevailed in the elections, winning 42 seats out of the 102 available seats, with PANGU winning 24. Despite this, PANGU formed a coalition government with Somare, showcasing what would be his oft repeated political mastery in years to come.

In February 1973, Somare, as the Chief Minister, announced in the House of Assembly an economic and social program which came to be known as the **Eight Point Plan.** The plan provided for:

- a rapid increase in the proportion of the economy under the control of Papua New Guineans;
- a more equal distribution of economic benefits including equalization of income among people and equalization of services among different parts of the country;
- decentralization of economic activity and an emphasis on agricultural development, village industry and internal trade;
- an emphasis on small-scale artisan, service and business activity;

- a more self-reliant economy less dependent upon imported goods and services;
- an increasing capacity to meet government expenditure from locally raised revenue;
- a rapid increase in the equal and active participation of women in all forms of economic and social activity; and
- government control and investment in those sectors of the economy where control was necessary to achieve the desired kind of development.

This plan was essentially the PANGU economic policy as composed in 1968.

Cecil did not contest the 1972 Elections for reasons unknown to me, but he became a principal advisor to Somare, the Chief Minister.

On the 1st of December 1973, self-governing status was attained.

The Constitutional Planning Committee under the Chairmanship of John Momis presented its Final Report in August 1974. This report was debated into early 1975.

The Justice Minister at the time was Ebia Olewale, and he and his department, legislative draftsman, CJ Lynch, in particular, in conjunction with officials from the Chief Minister's Department and Office, worked on amending and producing the various drafts of the *Constitution*.

The *Constitution* in its final form was predicated on five National Goals and Directive Principles as referred to in the **Preamble to the Constitution** – *Integral Human Development, Equality and Participation, National Sovereignty and Self Reliance, Natural Resources and Environment*, and *Papua New Guinea ways*.

These National Goals and Directive Principles were **heavily linked to the original Eight Point Plan.**

Cecil finally, was also credited with **writing the Preamble to the Constitution;**

*"**WE, THE PEOPLE** OF PAPUA NEW GUINEA—*

- *united in one nation*
- *pay homage to the memory of our ancestors—the source of our strength and origin of our combined heritage*
- *acknowledge the worthy customs and traditional wisdoms of our people—which have come down to us from generation to generation; and*
- *pledge ourselves to guard and pass on to those who come after us our noble traditions and the Christian principles that are ours now*

By authority of our inherent right as ancient, free, and independent peoples;

We, the people, do now establish this sovereign nation and declare ourselves, under the guiding hand of God, to be the Independent State of Papua New Guinea.

And we assert, by virtue of that authority;

- *that all power belongs to the people – acting through their duly elected representatives;*
- *that respect for the dignity of the individual and community interdependence are basic principles of our society;*
- *that we guard with our lives our national identity, integrity and self-respect;*
- *that we reject violence and seek consensus as a means of solving our common problems; and*
- *that our national wealth, won by honest, hard work be equitably shared by all*

We do now therefore declare, that we, having resolved to enact a Constitution for the Independent State of Papua New Guinea,

And acting through our Constituent Assembly on 15 August 1975,

Hereby establish, adopt, and give to ourselves this Constitution to come into effect on **Independence Day**, *that is, 16 September 1975.*

In so doing we, the people of Papua New Guinea, set before ourselves these national goals and directive principles that underlie our Constitution:—…"

You will always note a common thread that can be traced all the way back to the foundation work at Kwato, that of building **self-reliance** in a people to **prepare them to manage and determine their own affairs.**

In May of 1975 the Members of the House of Assembly convened as the National Constituent Assembly and debated and accepted the *Constitution.*

The Independent State of Papua New Guinea came into being on the 16th of September 1975.

In 1972, Sir Cecil Abel was awarded an OBE for services to politics in Papua New Guinea, and in 1982, aged 79, was awarded his Knighthood. He died in 1994 and was buried at Kwato Island, like his father.

Albert Maori Kiki, Tony Voutas, Pita Lus, Barry Holloway, Paul Lapun, Cecil Abel, Michael Somare, Oala-Oala Rarua – House Of Assembly, 1967.

Benoma Dagoela and Russell Abel translating the New Testament into the Suau language (published in 1962).

The view from the 'big house' on Kwato over to Logeia Island.

Chapter 6

Two Plane Crashes

Chris Abel stared at the unmistakable boot print in the mud at his feet and he almost collapsed. They had somehow, disastrously, come full circle. After slowly making their way to the bottom of another rocky valley, the raggedy group had found yet another dead end and had painstakingly climbed the lowest section of the ridge to the right. They had not eaten for five days now and were exhausted. Clambering down to the next valley they had again followed the strategy of descending, trying to find the Kokoda Valley. Instead, they were back in the previous location. It was hard not to panic. He turned to the other three. Thankfully they were hardened, tough men, not new to the territory conditions.

"Sit down for a minute guys," he said, before breaking the bad news to them.

Chris Abel, the 29-year-old Agricultural Officer for Kokoda Subdistrict, Tony Pryke, the Assistant District Officer, Wallace 'Soca' Kienzle, and a young patrol officer flown in from Woitape, all sat in the middle of the jungle on the Owen Stanley mountain range, shoulders slumped and heads drooped. The rain kept its constant, endless drizzle. They were completely and utterly lost. Chris had been struggling for some days to suppress his worst fears. They burst through now and he thought of the two boys at Kokoda, Charlie and Owen, who were two and one years old. They would grow up not knowing their father.

"At approximately 1325 hours Eastern Standard Time on 26 September 1970, a Piper PA23-250 Aztec aircraft, registered VH-SPM, collided with the precipitous face of a ravine, 490 feet below the main line of a ridge, on the eastern slopes of Mt. Scratchley in the Territory of Papua. The aircraft was engaged on a charter flight for the carriage of passengers and baggage from Kokoda to Port Moresby. The aircraft reported its departure from Kokoda but, when it did not arrive at Port Moresby, search and rescue procedures were initiated.

The wreckage was sighted on 1 October 1970 in dense rainforest, 10 100 feet above mean sea level. At first, the efforts of ground rescue parties to reach the wreckage were frustrated by extremely bad weather conditions, the high altitude, and precipitous terrain. Thirteen more days elapsed before a member of a mountain rescue party reached the accident site to find that the aircraft had been destroyed by impact forces and the pilot and that the three passengers on board had suffered fatal injuries. **(Accident Investigation Report, Special Investigation Report 70-5, Air Safety Investigation Branch, Department of Civil Aviation Australia. April 1971).**

Two Australian RAAF helicopters (rotary wing aircraft were transferred to the army in 1986) were at Kokoda at the time, presumably for training exercises. They immediately commenced an aerial search, following first reports of the crash, but did not locate the site until six days later.

A rescue party of volunteers was assembled following the crash sighting. This comprised the ADO, Tony Pryke, the youngest son of war hero Bert Kienzle, Wallace 'Soca' Kienzle, Agricultural Officer, Chris Abel, and a patrol officer who flew in from Woitape.

They were all government administration staff except for 'Soca' Kienzle.

(Herbert 'Bert' Thomson Kienzle had come to New Guinea in 1927 to work for Papua Rubber Plantations Pty. Ltd. He returned to Kokoda after the war and developed a magnificent rubber and cattle property which he called Mamba Estates. He was awarded an MBE for his military service, and a CBE for his civil service to Papua. As a result of reforms following independence in 1975, his plantation estate was compulsorily acquired in 1979, and he retired to Queensland. He died on 7 January 1988 while on a visit to Sydney.)

All of these men were quite territory seasoned, though of relatively young ages. 'Soca' had grown up at Kokoda and was credited as the youngest white man to have walked the Kokoda Trail when he was thirteen years old. Chris had grown up in the Territory and had spent years walking the bush as a 'didiman'.

On the 8th of October the two Bell 47 Sioux choppers lifted off with two passengers each. These are light choppers with only three seats and a cargo carrying capacity of the equivalent of two more people. This would explain why the first two loads were so sparse of rations and equipment, which led to the ensuing hardships when the choppers could not return with further supplies.

One of the pilots was twenty-seven-year-old Malcom 'Kela' Smith who was fresh out of the Vietnam War where he had been awarded the Distinguished Flying Cross. In 1969, he was posted to New Guinea where he eventually had a successful career in business and politics until his death in 2021.

The aircraft could only carry two passengers and limited cargo per trip. This meant that with the four-man rescue party, there were only two tents, some bush-knives, files, a radio, and some rations scrounged together by the volunteers themselves. There was a combination of factors that came into play here, including the misbehavior of the weather, that resulted in what possibly could have been four more unnecessary fatalities.

It was on a weekend when the crash was sighted and so the public service was not particularly alert. The Bell 47s were limited in load capacity resulting in inadequate supplies from a single run. It was presumed that the helicopters would be able to service the crash location with more equipment and supplies as needed. The battery to the communication radio provided was flat. Then the weather played its hand. The instructions were to try to get to the plane wreckage and effect a rescue, if possible, and then construct a chopper landing pad for the extractions and full investigations to continue.

At around midday in relatively good weather, they approached Mount Scratchley at 10 000 feet. The bubble Bell 47s were buffeted at such proximity to a wind-swept, undulated terrain. The men were immediately reminded of how the temperature plummets at these elevations.

They could only find sufficient open ground to discharge at several hundred metres higher than the crash location, beyond the tree line. It was jagged and rocky with a few twisted trees. The choppers hurriedly disgorged and thumped back away into the distance.

"Be back in a minute mate." Mal had said through the earphones.

The men, led by Tony Pryke, picked their way carefully down towards the tree line carrying their cargo on their backs. Making their way through the trees, they came to the edge of a ravine. It had begun to drizzle now, and peering over they could barely make out a scattering of white patches representing pieces of fuselage and cargo in a trail into the end of the ravine and the main body of the plane. 'Soca' went over the edge and descended as far as he could before returning to say they needed climbing ropes to go any further.

"The wreckage was located 10 100 feet above mean sea level on the north-western side of a ridge which runs in a north-easterly direction from the Owen Stanley Range. The top of the ridge immediately above the impact point is 10 590 feet above mean sea level. The main impact occurred at the end of a blind, steep-sided ravine and against a 60-degree slope which extends upwards to the top of the ridge. The area in which the accident occurred is uninhabited and covered by thick jungle growth. Access to the main wreckage was extremely difficult and was made from the ridge above the accident site. The descent of the last 100 feet was achieved only with the aid of ropes."

"This was not a survivable accident." **(Accident Investigation Report, Special Investigation Report 70-5, Air Safety Investigation Branch, Department of Civil Aviation Australia. April 1971).**

It was mid-afternoon now and the rain was getting heavier and heavier. The clouds had descended and the temperature continued to drop.

Tony told them to get the tents up, establish radio contact and try to light a fire before dark. He would locate the best landing site.

About an hour later they had realized the radio did not work, there would be no fire because of a lack of any dry tinder, and the helicopters would not be returning that day.

It was bone chillingly cold that night and they forgot any inhibitions and took turns cuddling each other to maintain body heat.

There were only a couple of tins of bully beef, a packet of bacon, and some navy biscuits that Chris had managed to throw into a bag. Inside his shirt, against his skin, he carried his usual tobacco makings and a box of matches inside an old plastic rice packet.

The next day they commenced building a log platform on the top of a ridge to provide a landing pad for the helicopters as the slope into and around the edges of the ravine was too steep. They worked all day through the rain. As they chopped and dragged the timber to the site, they attempted to identify any dry wood for the fire. Chris who had always prided himself in his bushcraft and ability to light a fire under any conditions . was nonplussed as he lit each match and blew the kindling unsuccessfully. The rain continued, no choppers came and dusk fell.

Incredibly, this cycle continued for five days before they completely ran out of food. The landing pad had been completed and it was a matter of waiting out the rain and cloud cover.

'Soca' had been relating stories at night of his father's war exploits and also how he had walked up and down these mountains on hiking trips. He said it shouldn't be too difficult to walk out.

On day seven, after two days without food and no respite from the weather, they collectively decided to walk out to save themselves. They would simply follow ridge and valley in an ever-descending manner until they reached the Kokoda Valley. They estimated that it should take no more than two days.

A full six days later they sat slumped, exhausted, and lost after going in circles and finding themselves at dead- end gullies or the end of ridges that were too steep to climb down safely.

The other frustrating thing was the inability to find edible plants or small mammals that you would find at lower altitudes. Thankfully, there was always an abundance of water which was a blessing, and a curse. With blunt bush knives they could not even get at the inner pith through the tough skin of the black palm plants that they found. They still had not been able to light a fire and Chris was down to his last two matches.

The tents had been left behind as they were too heavy and they had been sleeping wet and on open ground. It was freezing and they were starving to death. Chris had lost nine kilograms from his already wiry frame and 'Soca' had lost sixteen kilograms. They were skinny, covered in mud and scratches and were barely talking any more. For the first time these hardened and generally positive and cheery men began to consider the worst.

The thought of his two young boys overwhelmed him, and in this moment of despair, Chris explained that, he **"cast his burden to the Lord."**

He looked at Tony directly in the eyes and said, "We make one last climb with our remaining strength and then wait there no matter what."

Tony had been suffering from dysentery and was the worst of the four. They dragged themselves up and virtually crawled up the nearest ridge for the next two hours.

At home in Kokoda, Chris's mother, Sheila Abel, had flown in from Port Moresby where she worked as a teacher since losing her husband, Russell, in 1965. She was thinking she may have lost her eldest son as well. It had been almost two weeks now since her son had been gone. Her daughter-in-law, Barbara, had been cooking every day, believing her husband would turn up at any time. She refused to believe the stories from the locals about dogs the size of horses that lived in the mountains and ate stray humans.

Finally, the missing group broke out at the top of their ridge of last hope, and there in the distance was the glorious sight of the township of Kokoda. With his last two matches Chris, was finally able to get a roaring fire going on which they heaped green foliage to get some smoke billowing. Searching around, he discovered a large nest of ant eggs that they were all able to share. It was their first food in over a week.

There was an immediate response from the choppers at Kokoda and the first thing they did was a food drop. They then landed at nearby Kanga Village and, before long, the village people came noisily up the ridge.

They were back at Kokoda that afternoon and two young boys ran to their dad and grabbed his muddy legs in glee.

Thirty-nine years later on the 11th of August 2009 at 11:11am, Captain Jannie Moala was overheard by Air Traffic Control in Port Moresby saying to another aircraft,

"Thank you very much, monin lon yu."

These were the last communications heard from flight CG4682. Shortly afterwards, the Airlines PNG, de Havilland Twin Otter crashed into the mountain side above Isurava Village within the Kokoda Valley. The Kokoda Gap was heavily clouded and Captain Moala and her co-pilot, First Officer Rodney Souka, were attempting to descend into the Kokoda Valley.

The investigation concluded that the accident was probably a controlled flight into terrain; that is, an otherwise airworthy aircraft was unintentionally flown into terrain, with little or no awareness by the crew of the impending collision.

The aircraft was carrying eleven passengers and two crew. The passengers included eight Australian tourists on their way to trek the Kokoda Track, two tour guides (one Australian and one Papua New Guinean) from the No Roads Expeditions tour company, and a Japanese tourist. The crash was discovered the following day. No-one survived.

As I trudged up the 'Top Town' hill, in Alotau, on the morning of the 12th, in my heavy boots, doing my preparations for the Kokoda Track, my phone rang. It was Peter Vincent, the CEO of the Tourism Promotion Authority.

"Minister, I have some bad news."

As I listened to his explanation my heart sank. The Owen Stanley Mountains that had come so close to taking my father, had claimed another plane. The two Papua New Guinean pilots included a young female captain. It was still a pioneering field for women in our country. It was devastating for the families and for our fledgling tourism industry.

I was the Culture and Tourism Minister at the time and had been drumming up support inside and outside of Parliament for a historic walk of the Kokoda Track to raise funds for the local communities and witness first hand our country's No.1 tourist attraction. While the Track had been walked by several Members of the Australian Parliament, it had never been walked fully by a PNG MP or Minister, let alone the Tourism Minister.

It was with some degree of trepidation that I boarded an Airlines PNG Twin Otter two weeks later on the 28th of August in Port Moresby, recommenced flights into Kokoda, and stuck to my commitment to visit Kokoda and walk the Track.

I had to convince Hacy to miss her netball grand final by saying that this was a once in a lifetime experience. She often reminds me of moments like when I was carefully splashing my face at Camp 2000 on top of the spine of Papua New Guinea. It was absolutely freezing in the early morning fog. She took a few steps back and launched herself into the freezing water right beside me. After much cursing I had no option but to jump in as well. I would remind her how I towed her up every mountain with my towel and would stop and wait every ten minutes for her to catch her breath!

We visited every location possible in Kokoda and I had to stop for a ceremony and speech at literally every village on the 95-kilometre track. Several times I was 'ambushed' by the villagers and 'locked up' in a staged drama to lament all their lack of development and unfulfilled expectations. Many of them remembered my father and his time as an Agricultural Officer there.

I had read up on all the history so I knew the significance of every point in relation to the war. I shed a tear at the beautiful memorial at Isurava on the climb out of the Kokoda Valley. I thought of the recent crash victims as well as the young soldiers who sacrificed their lives far away from their homes. It was a rainy, cloudy day just like on the days when the **two planes crashed** into these very mountains. I could almost hear the banzai cries of the Japanese soldiers as they charged relentlessly. They appeared to many of the Australian soldiers as giants of men, no doubt fostered by their undefeated status and fearsome reputation.

Walking through the jungle tracks I swear that the birds were mimicking the rattling fire of the Vickers machine guns that they have adopted from the Second World War.

It took us a full ten days of trekking over 90 kilometres of very rugged landscape, led by the wonderful Fuzzy Wuzzy Expeditions and a group of amazing people from the Kokoda Track Authority, the Tourism Promotion Authority, and the Australian DFAT. Friendships are most certainly forged out of shared adversity.

It seemed like a miracle when we finally arrived at the river below Owers Corner on the outskirts of Port Moresby, and there appeared a sprinkling of cold soft drinks and beer on the river bed, just below the surface. To think that the record for traversing the Track is just seventeen hours by a young porter from Kokoda!

Kokoda and the Kokoda Track represent so many elements of our history and forging as a nation. It is a sacred place for this reason and for the burial place that it is. It is certainly a part of my family history as well.

As I closed my tired eyes each night at camp, I knew that I would soon hear the distant and close voices of the many souls that were a part of these mountains now. They would blend with the singing of the boys around the campfire. I held no fear, I had come to pay my respects to this place.

Air Investigation Report 1970.

Captain Herbert (Bert) Thomson Kienzle during the Second World War.

Charles K. Abel, Chris Abel, Owen Abel, Kokoda 1970.

Chapter 7

Rich Harvest

I can remember sitting with Sir John Luke, who was the Governor for Milne Bay at the time, and I was the Deputy Prime Minister, Treasurer, and MP for Alotau Open.

"Money is everything!" he bellowed to me in his customary belligerent manner when pressing his argument.

"Money is not everything, Sir John." I replied. "It is absolutely necessary in life to meet basic needs, but beyond that it is only a tool to get the important things done."

"Rubbish!" he laughed.

I say this at the opening of this chapter to emphasize a vital factor that underpinned the amazing success story which arose from a strange marriage of convenience between a missionary and a businessman, who both ultimately became Knights of the Realm in their service to the people of Papua New Guinea.

In 1972, my father, Sir Christopher Abel (just 'Chris' in those days), was a 'didiman' or agricultural officer with the Australian Administration of the Territory of Papua, based at Kokoda. He had served initially in the Mekeo/Kuni area west of Port Moresby, commencing in 1963 at Bakoiudu (50 kilometres inland from Yule Island) after graduating from Dookey Agricultural College in Victoria, Australia. He was doing what he loved, working in the bush, training and supporting local people to grow cash crops, establishing cooperative societies, and serving what he has always felt was his own country, Papua New Guinea.

He had met my mother, Barbara Hapea Kauvu, at Bereina, the headquarters of the Kairuku Subdistrict, in 1967. After a prickly time negotiating around her very strict and serious father, a carpenter and lay preacher, they had a traditional Western wedding and I appeared on the scene at Veifa-a Catholic Health Centre on the 24th of September 1968, after much resistance and giving mum a terrible time in labour.

My middle name, Kauvu, comes from my maternal grandfather, Kauvu Haro, who I got to know a little later in life, confirming his serious and stern character, which was in remarkable contrast to the relaxed, bubbly and warm character that was Evelove Kauvu, my grandmother. Both were from Iokea Village on the eastern border of Gulf Province.

Kauvu, who wore a white laplap and leather belt on Sundays and administered from the Bible, was not averse though to dabbling in some more traditional activities as it seemed to me on occasions.

Mum and Dad had left us in the care of Aunty Liz at Alotau, to go on a trip to the United States of America and Canada. This was actually a very rare luxury which I don't think ever happened again. Dad was investigating his spiritual connections with the American Indians, and fascination with the wild west of North American history.

I would ride my BMX bike every day after school up the gravel road, from KB Mission to Goilanai, which was up on the ridge overlooking the bay, to be with my grandparents, and often spent the night or weekends with them. Most times I would take the shortcut directly from the main road up a steep bush track carrying my bike. On one rainy occasion I slipped in the red clay of Goilanai Ridge and found the next day that I could not walk! I remember poor Uncle Murray (dad's younger brother) carrying me from the car to the X-ray room at Alotau General Hospital. I was deposited soon after at my grandfather's house and lay there under his silent and stern glare. They could barely speak English and after a lot of verbal instructions in the Toaripi language to my uncles, Daniel and Peter, and Bubu Evelove, he folded his legs beside me and took the cup of water from Evelove. There began the familiar singing and chanting with his breath close over the water. He paused and dramatically spat in the water and handed the cup to me.

Unfortunately, I had no choice, and slowly raised the cup, closed my eyes and drained it. Two days later I was walking again with no idea what caused the crippling, or healed my legs.

My brother, Owen Russell Abel, was born on the 16th of August 1969, during the South Pacific Games in Port Moresby. Dad explained to me on numerous occasions that his plan was always to bring us 'home' to Milne Bay to benefit from the historical awareness of the family and be close to Kwato.

In 1972, Chris applied for the position of Provincial Development Bank Officer to Milne Bay and was posted to Alotau. Again, he relished the work, helped families, business groups, and individuals obtain loans to support their agriculture projects, boat building, and trade-stores.

He travelled far and wide in the maritime province on little wooden workboats, building new relationships, and meeting childhood friends. Having grown up on Kwato and being fluent in the Suau language (he was later to publish the Suau Dictionary), he had a special affinity for the Suau, Bwanabwaba, and Tawala people, that he was to maintain throughout his life.

In 1973, we had two visits from an enterprising, young Swiss/French man by the name of John Luke Crittin. He was a rice farmer and crocodile hunter who had met Dad in their earlier adventures. Over some rolled Drum tobacco cigarettes, glasses of Johnny Walker whisky, and games of chess, there was some serious talk going on between the two friends.

I can say now as I write these words that I have come to know these two gentlemen intimately. Chris is probably the most genuinely selfless person that I know. In terms of his life work, and plans and intentions, there is no doubt whatsoever that he was motivated primarily by an innate sense of wanting to help others. He is reserved and self-deprecating. John Luke, on the other hand is loud, confronting, borderline narcissistic, and annoyingly pragmatic.

We used to go swimming on the weekends as kids at 'Rattley Bridge' at Waema, between Alotau and Gurney Airport. It was named because of the clattering it made when you drove over the marston matting metal surface, taken from the No1 Airstrip (Gurney) from the Second World War. This has long since been replaced by a concrete bridge and the general public would not consider swimming in such a place today.

I was still learning to swim properly and was cautiously splashing on the edges of the rain swollen river.

"Legume!" John Luke called out to me from the bank where he was sitting smoking a cigarette. He had a nickname for me and I for him.

I looked at him suspiciously, knowing him too well. "Yes Mataglas?" (reading glasses).

He had risen and waded into the water. He grabbed me under the armpits and threw me into the middle of the river. I came up coughing and spluttering. I almost drowned that day but learned to swim.

The germination and actualization of the business venture that came to be Masurina is an example of how an idea, manifested out of good intentions and focused on with a passion, can attract the necessary elements and circumstances to make it a reality.

Chris Abel had returned home after ten years of service in the government in order to raise his children in Milne Bay, and with a deep desire to do something for the people there. He carried on his conscience a heavy sense of historical context and inherited duty.

His involvement with the Kwato Church was immediate and constant. He attended and participated in the spiritual life, often speaking at the Russell Abel Memorial Church at KB Mission, and chaired the Church Council for a term. I can recall countless Sunday services where my mind would wander off as all the preaching and singing was in the Suau language. One of my great regrets was growing up in a home where Mum's first language was Toaripi and Dad's was Suau, and we did not learn to speak either properly. They can both speak Police Motu and the Roro language as well.

There were constant trips between Alotau and Kwato Island as he tried venture after venture to revive education and commercial activities under the church at Kwato to spark activity and employment.

There came later on the large real estate development on church plantation land at KB, on the edge of Alotau. Again, the intention was to empower the church, and the original landowners, and avoid the land being taken over by squatters.

In 1974, the township of Alotau was in its infancy as the provincial capital, having being designated as such in the late 1960s when it was transferred from Samarai Island. Samarai was historically one of the three major settlements in Papua New Guinea from the colonial era, the other two being Port Moresby and Rabaul. The major businesses of the time, Steamships Trading Company and Burns Philp, still dominated the commercial landscape and maintained significant shipping and trading operations, including at Samarai. Alotau at this point was a single street, with three Chinese tradestores and a sprinkling of public servant housing. There were no significant local companies or businesses at this time.

Masurina commenced operations in 1974, one year before Independence, from a rented Tea Shop in the fledgling town of Alotau with no capital and big dreams.

The first meeting was attended by thirteen interested people, including the foundation shareholders – Mila Walo, Leve Mwado, Chris Abel, Maurice Halabei, Gerald Allan, Hilary Gorio and John Luke. Others included Iairo Lasaro, who under the mentoring of the company would become Chairman of the Board for a time, and was elected in 1987, 1992 and 1997 as the Member of Parliament for Alotau Open. He would eventually serve as Deputy Prime Minister. John Luke would be elected Governor for Milne Bay in 2007 and 2017.

The name Masurina as proposed by Chris meant *'rich harvest'* in the Suau language. In 1989, he wrote;

"The idea of Masurina as a local company to provide a counterbalance to the foreign business interests in the province, was felt to be urgent at this time. The plans were to go into areas of development which were beyond the capacity of local individuals or family groups. This vision has continued to expand and now includes resource development activities such as agro-forestry, mining, marine produce, and in fact, any activity which has an impact of any kind on Milne Bay people and resources."

"Masurina (wealth) for Milne Bay people is to be shared. The shareholding of the company is 100 percent owned by Papua New Guineans, and especially Milne Bay people. Today, the number of shareholders has gone well over 600. Out of the 600 shareholdings we have church groups and local government councils who also have shares in the company. Considering the churches and the local

government councils, group membership in excess of the actual shareholder members gives rise to a wide spread of benefits throughout the Milne Bay Province."

From 1974 to 1999, which was its 25th anniversary, Masurina Limited grew to be a public company with ten million Kina in assets (K30m in today's money), over 600 shareholders, 300 employees, with diversified operations in marine produce exports, prawning and fishing, shipping, accommodation and hospitality, slipway services and marine chandlery, construction and furniture manufacture, real estate and property rentals, and financial and trustee services. Attempts had been made to diversify into agriculture and alluvial mining.

In a relatively small economy like that of Milne Bay, the footprint and impact of these activities was enormous. The dividends paid, employment and training, extension of credit services so people could have boats and fuel to harvest and sell their marine produce, boat networks that provided shipping services to remote islands, touched thousands of lives. Simple things like provision of free transit accommodation for island people visiting Alotau made a big impression.

Importantly, the philosophy of local people having a genuine ownership stake in the economy was actualized. They were able to see that it was possible to compete with the foreign businesses and succeed. The company was always majority owned by the local shareholders until the latter years when it became apparent that successive generations preferred to sell their shares.

The practical reality in bringing this to realization was the need for a hard-nosed businessman. John Luke was the vital ingredient here. He demonstrated the necessary planning, work ethic, and discipline that is required to run a modern business. It was important for the local directors and management to see and learn from this. He went on to be the elected Governor for Milne Bay on two separate occasions, and was Knighted for his services to business and politics. He, like many others, was drawn to Milne Bay by a humble man with a vision.

An element that is worth expanding on was the development of part of the KB Mission coconut plantation into an integrated suburb in the Alotau township.

The KB Mission is part of the Kwato Church, and the associated lands were given by the original landowners of Mutuyuwa to the church to support the work of the church, including the training of the local people, and to protect the land from acquisition by colonial interests, particularly planters.

By the late 1960s, the church had lost momentum for reasons which were only compounded by the death of Russell Abel in 1965, and participated in the amalgamation of the LMS churches to form the *Papua Ekelesia*. In 1968, the Papua Ekelesia, with the Methodist Church, formed the United Church of Papua New Guinea. There was a change of heart by elements of the Kwato Church in the mid-1970s, and after a protracted battle and secession in 1977, and an Act of Parliament —

the *Kwato Church Incorporation Act* 1979, the church was re-established and its lands returned.

In the meantime, much of these land holdings were neglected, and in the case of KB Mission, overgrown and being gradually populated by squatters.

During Russell's time, the northern portion around Cameron Plateau had been given to the Administration for the establishment of a secondary school. Cameron Secondary School and the KB Compound suburb were developed on this land.

On the southern seaside portion was the church's headquarters and where Chris was heavily involved, on returning to Alotau, in the establishment of the Kwato Saugere Guest House, and eventually the KB Primary School and KB Elementary School. An older institution, the Kwato Vocational School was across the road in the central portion of the KB Plantation land. The balance of this portion was in danger of being lost.

With a capital injection from Masurina, the land input from the Church, and the reintroduction of the original landowners with free equity, the KB Development Company and subdivision was commenced. This project realized 600 blocks of land for development, homes, employment and an organized and formal expansion of the town. Today, KB Developments is majority owned by the landowners with the church as the minority shareholder. It has a substantial property portfolio and a construction company that has pre-emptive development rights on any land that is sold in the subdivision. It provides a substantial income back to the church and landowners, and performs many community service obligations.

I have witnessed sustained effort over twenty years by my father to this project, including several court cases, and accusations. He has always stood for the interests of the church, and the landowners in particular, and they have stood with him, represented by a wonderful woman leader in Setima Manuega.

A man can truly be judged by the outcomes of his sustained efforts over time. The tireless efforts of this man have demonstrated an amazing sense of obligation and duty to the service of others.

In a similar vein, Dad spent hours and hours of his time supporting the landowners of the Toudikwa subdivision, on the eastern boundary of Alotau Town, to register their land under the new *Incorporated Land Group Act*, and *Customary Land Registration Act*. Toudikwa became one of the first examples of formal land registration where the landowners retain the head titles to the land, and then subdivide and lease to customers, who pay a capital sum and ongoing monthly rentals to the landowners. The challenge for the government has been how to do this under a 'security of tenure' system for the leaseholders, and for banks to lend against.

The landowners of Toudikwa have asked that the main avenue of the subdivision be named after Sir Christopher Abel.

Sir Christopher Charles Abel received Independence Medals in 1985, 2000, and 2005, and an OBE in 2007. He was Knighted in 2018.

(Sir) John Luke Crittin, 1999.

**The Directors of Masurina in 1993, P. Moyaru, T. Deboeamina, S Zychewicz,
H. Igayoma, G. Allan (standing), C. Abel, L. Mwado,
J Crittin (seated).**

Masurina Limited, Annual Report 1992.

Chapter 8

During a Snowstorm

It is Sunday the 16th of October 2022, as I sit here in the hospital room with my father lying prone with tubes sticking out of him. Sir Christopher Charles Abel is suffering from cancer, and it is a slow and inexorable process. I cried and cried when we got the news of the recurrence of the cancer, after Dad's initial bout. I absorbed the grief and pain for my father of the moment, but more so the months ahead. I asked my dear wife why a man with so much good in his heart, who has only helped people all his life, is condemned so? I asked my Lord the same question. (Dad passed away at 7:03 a.m. on Monday the 5th December 2022 in Alotau, and his funeral was attended by at least two thousand people).

There are three chapters about my father and the lessons I have learned from him. He has overwhelmingly been a force of love and good in our lives, and we love him fiercely for that. We love our mother dearly as well, and she is a proud and strong woman, who has undoubtedly given me much of my confidence and self-belief. However, to say it has been all good would be untruthful.

I woke to a crash on the floor above. I was immediately filled with dread as I heard my mother's shrill voice screaming at my father. I looked over at my two little brothers whose beds were to the left of me. Owen was eight and Jeffrey was six. Their eyes were wide open.

There was another crash and I heard Dad's muffled words of pleading. There was more banging and yelling and I heard someone crash to the floor.

Jeffrey started crying. I went over and sat with my two siblings, and put my arms around them. "It's ok, just Mum and Dad quarrelling again, don't worry," I assured them.

"Go up and make sure Dad is ok please." said Owen. I looked into his worried face, took a deep breath, "I will. Just don't worry, ok?"

As I slowly took the steep stairs that connected our downstairs bedroom to the living room upstairs, I knew the all too familiar scene. I would find my mother drunk and hysterical, and my father angry and desperate.

On so many occasions I had cried and pleaded with them. The tears had dried up, but I was scared, angry, and resentful. I loved them both so, but resented my mother for her behaviour, and my father for putting up with it. I hated the stink of alcohol and cigarettes, the screaming, the violence. I hated the dread every time Mum went out with her friends. I hated being embarrassed when Mum abused Dad at social occasions. I had nightmares that Mum would, one day, kill Dad, and we would be abandoned.

As I stepped into the warzone upstairs, I could see Mum sobbing with her head in her hands, I looked around for Dad. He was slumped in a lounge chair holding on to his side. Mum had stabbed him, "Dad!!" I shouted, as the tears came again.

My brothers and I, and my sister, who arrived the following year, are the product of a mixed-race marriage. My parents are (were) both wonderful people with amazing individual qualities. They survived a tumultuous marriage, and I have no doubt that they love (loved) us and love (loved) each other.

I write this chapter about my father, and fatherhood in general, and the lessons I learned from him. It goes without saying that the most important job we have is the role that we play as parents. The father is the head of the household. He plays the critical role in the stability of the family, and the example he displays to his sons and daughters in the way he treats their mother, and shoulders his responsibilities.

Sir Cecil Abel, my grand-uncle (elder brother of my grandfather, Russell Abel), was one of the first white men to formally marry a local girl. She was an amazingly warm and loving lady by the name of Semi Bwagagaia, from Dawadawa, in Milne Bay. Being the mid-1900s, they faced the stigma of the times where, despite there being many mixed-race children, rarely did a white man put his name to a local woman in marriage.

It's very common now, but even when my Dad did the right thing and married Mum in 1968, when she was expecting me, it was still relatively rare. These men made a commitment and stuck to their marriages and responsibilities as fathers.

It was not until I started at boarding school in Toowoomba, in 1981, that I really learned about racism, and that there was supposedly something to be ashamed about for having black blood. I remember having a fight with one of the law students in our residence while at university (it wasn't really a fight as I was rock solid and he was a skinny, smart-arse law student that I pinned up on the wall with one hand), about the difference in institutional racism in South Africa and Australia. Somehow, he ended up giving my parents as an example of racism of the colonial kind.

Chris Abel was born ***during a snowstorm,*** on the 18th of May 1941, in Dunedin, New Zealand. The Second World War had spread from Europe to the Pacific, and his dad, Russell, then went back to Sydney to enlist, but was not accepted because of health reasons and his age, and set to work digging war bunkers instead.

Dad had a rather frugal upbringing during the war years in New Zealand, or immediate post-war years at Kwato. In Dunedin, they stayed with his grandparents from his mother's side. It was difficult times, and people relied on ration coupons for food. Doctor William J. Porteous, his grandfather, was running his own practice, but there were few patients and little money. They were Scottish immigrants. Dr. Porteous was a medical doctor and Presbyterian missionary who took part in special deputation to India in 1908 to search for a suitable mission area for the New Zealand Presbyterian Church. He served as a doctor for the Punjab Mission, Shahabad, which relocated to Jagadhri, Northern Punjab, until his resignation in 1926. He married Edith Rayner in 1909.

We had the wonderful blessing to be taken care of by our paternal grandmother, Bubu Sheila, when we were at high school on the Sunshine Coast in the early 1980s, and you could see her frugality born out of two world wars, and a missionary life in India. If there was any time that, perchance, we had two sources of protein for dinner, like chicken and fish, she would say that it was a 'terrible luxury'.

The frugality of life on Kwato was made up for by the bountiful natural surroundings and the extended Kwato family that they were a part of. This entailed social activities, games, education, and church life, beyond that of an ordinary childhood. The Suau language challenged English as Dad's first language as a result.

His father, Russell Abel, was very active in the running of the Mission, and was often away on duty in the outstations. Russell had also been away during the war years. Dad then went to Christchurch in 1954 to start in Grade Five at Cashmere Primary School, from there to Carey Grammar in Melbourne, Geelong Grammar, and then Dookey Agricultural College in 1960.

Russell did write loving letters to his son, but there was an absence and a lack of physical affection from his father that Dad noted.

I always noted that Dad, while being the most loving person, had difficulty with physical affection. We, his children, would throw ourselves upon him but he was always a bit restrained in return.

I remember being rather taken aback one time when I was trying to take a picture of Dad and Mum with a polaroid instant camera on one of our boat trips and he put his arm around her. I had never really seen (or heard) physical intimacy between them.

My parents are both at fault for a marriage that caused great trauma to their children, largely because of a drinking problem that they refused to acknowledge and eliminate early on. Mum was very young when they married, and there was an evident social and cultural gap. My father brought a stoic, and logical approach to my mother, but perhaps this was not what she was craving. As time went by this frustration exploded when alcohol was added, and unfortunately became an all too regular occurrence in our home. As children, we saw a drunk and violent mother attacking our father on a regular basis. We saw our father also react violently after much provocation. We were filled with fear and frustration.

One of my major fears earlier, being the elder brother and having to deal with parents trying to hurt each other, was the prospect of somehow losing Dad.

I can remember asking so many times, if they could both stop drinking. It never happened despite assurances.

I have carried with me a sense of insecurity from my childhood, and my relationships with women were affected in the sense that I felt that they were trying to control me. As a result, I responded with alcohol and violence in my own marriage. I know my siblings have had their own struggles.

I have been blessed with a wife who has the wisdom and strength to confront issues and deal with them. Love requires tough decisions sometimes in order to address problems as early as possible. Bad behaviour that is tolerated and accepted because it's uncomfortable to deal with can create horrible distortions in people because they are not held accountable for their actions.

Many years ago, I decided alcohol does not fit into a proper family life and that I must start with myself.

Dad has always tried to act out of love and understanding. He is a selfless man who has literally helped thousands of people in his work in the public service, the private sector, and the church. Some people have taken advantage of his kind and gentle nature and desire to make everyone happy. Sometimes, tough love is needed, and certainly it was needed in our home when we were growing up, but we cannot hold it against such a man.

Chris Abel has been a wonderful father, grandfather and great grandfather. I am here in Milne Bay because of him. I have an Australian education because of him. I have an example of love, dedication, and service to others because of him. I have an example of appreciation and responsibility to a family legacy because of him. I will never meet his high standards, but am determined to keep trying.

**Sheila, Murray, Elizabeth, Russell and Christopher Abel.
Growing up on Kwato Island, c 1951.**

Rose (Kauvu) Arua, Barbara (Kauvu) Abel, Chris Abel, Murray Abel,
and Sheila Abel – Bereina 1968.

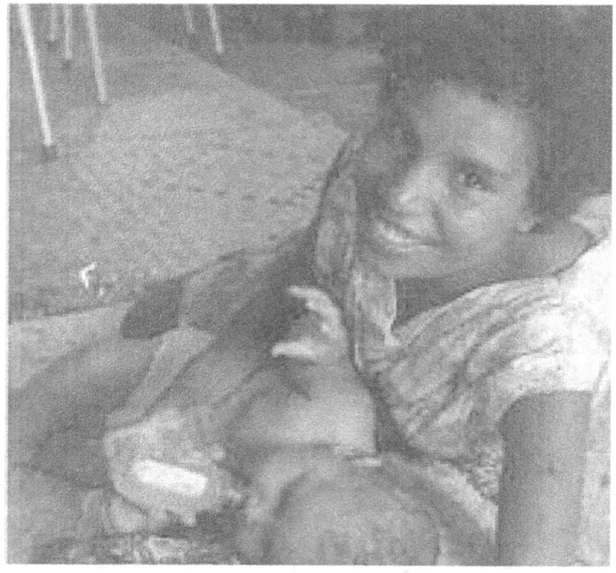

Charles K. Abel and Barbara Abel, 1968.

Chapter 9

Caramel Kids

I made my way slowly and painfully up the steps of the Chinese shop in the one street commercial centre of Alotau Town. I was nine years old, and it was 1977. This was the Chan's shop. I was best friends with Jason and Darren Chan, who attended correspondence school with me at the Ahioma Women's Centre under the tutelage of my grandmother, Ruth Sheila Abel.

I edged my way past the cashiers in front and along the lines of clothing and goods, past customers, until I came to the glass counter at the rear of the shop. Mrs. Renee Chan was her usual bustling, energetic, and buoyant self. She was rolling out cloth material for customers, directing staff, and cracking jokes. It was Mr. Andrew Chan who was always serious. Mrs. Chan was always so nice to us. I felt like an idiot.

Mrs. Chan looked up and with a smile said, "Hello Charlie, Jason is upstairs watching a video. I know you love videos!"

"Mrs. Chan, I have something to tell you." I said in a very low voice.

"Speak up son, I can't hear you. What's the matter?" She said.

I held out my little paw gingerly, and in it was a small fold up pocket knife. Mrs. Chan looked puzzled.

"I was in the shop with Jason and I took this from inside the shelf," I said. "My father told me to return it and apologize."

Mrs. Chan did not know what to say for a moment.

"I am very sorry Mrs. Chan. I will not do it again."

"You silly boy. Come in here and put it back. Don't do it again, ok?"

"No, Mrs. Chan."

We would go to Jason and Darren's house behind the shop every day after school to play snooker on the full-sized snooker table, watch cassette videos of "Happy Days" episodes, and "Hawaii Five O", for hours. We would play mah-jong, and eat salty plums, and salted red ginger. I would use the toilet and glance through Mr. Chan's Penthouse magazines thinking, how luxurious to read dirty magazines on the toilet.

We had no video deck, or snooker table, or Penthouse magazines at my house. If I took Darren and Jason to my home, they were bored in ten minutes.

When I looked across the paddock at my Uncle Murray and Aunty Cathy's place, there was a horse called Tula running around the paddock, a large swimming pool, a huge house, and manicured lawns. I used to wonder how come these people, who used to live downstairs in my own house, are richer than me now?

We were called the *'caramel kids'* (because of our colour), and people used to snicker and talk about my Mum's drinking problems.

I had a distinct sense of being of lesser means when growing up, which is strange, because we were much better off than the average person.

My father, together with John Luke, was building one of the biggest businesses in the province, but we were always cash strapped. Dad is the most frugal person in the world. He drove the oldest car and had holes in his shirt that Mum would patch.

I am a beneficiary of Dad's extensive music record collection in those days, and his book library. With no TV or video deck, I read everything I could get my hands on (including the odd Penthouse magazine). I scored the highest marks in English comprehension and creative writing throughout primary and secondary school largely because of this.

When Dad started bringing home self-help and get rich books like Napolean Hill's "Think and Grow Rich", Norma Vincent Peale's "The Power of Positive Thinking", Dale Carnegie's "How to Win Friends and Influence People", and Henry Thoreaus' "Walden", I devoured them as well.

One piece of advice I can give, is that if you want to improve your English and writing skills, as well as expand your knowledge, reading is a wonderful tool.

So, I developed a sense that, to be someone you had to make money and be rich. I had to think, plan, work hard, and make plenty of money! I thought that money was the most important thing in life.

My strength in high school was always the sciences, history, and English (and sport). I was above average but not the greatest with maths. My mind was made up though that I would be going to university and studying business.

We had the massive distraction of the surfing culture on the beautiful Sunshine Coast that I explain more in the chapter, **"Running for No Reason"**.

Despite the beach culture I refused to be consumed by it. My friends were all academically inclined, and university bound. I chose to associate with those I felt were of a like mind. We competed amongst each other for the best marks. Ultimately, in 1987, we did all make it to the University of Queensland (UQ), the top academic institution in the State of Queensland, and Scott Chapman achieved the highest tertiary entrance score, and did Veterinary Science, Justin Wilkie became a maths and science teacher, and Nathan Seefeld became a lecturer in Sports Psychology.

I chose Commerce as my first preference, but that required a 960 tertiary entrance score (highest being 990) at UQ. I had scored 930, so settled for my second preference of Economics, not wanting to go to any other university. This was to serve me well later when I became Treasurer for Papua New Guinea.

I did as many accounting and legal subjects as possible, and the resulting broader degree provided by the Economics foundation, I realized, later in life, was more suited to my truer self.

When we got to Uni, my father gave us the old blue Nissan L200 van and basically said, you're on your own now. Much of my Uni life was preoccupied trying to make enough money to pay my rent and buy food.

I picked strawberries, waited on tables, bounced at nightclubs, did house painting contracts, and worked long hours as a gym instructor.

For the first two years, we benefitted from a higher education allowance from the government, and were able to live in a United Church Hostel. This was where I struck up a relationship with a like-minded friend in Tim Johnson, who was doing Commerce at the University of Queensland (UQ).

When the government allowance was scrapped in 1988, Owen and I moved into a three-bedroom flat with six other students. We were living off lamb chops and noodles. I probably made it to 50 percent of my classes and would pass my exams by staying up all night cramming, take a couple of caffeine tablets, and do my best.

It was rather chaotic with Brett Evans practising his saxophone in the stairwell, Tim loudly making love to his girlfriend in the shower, and the rest of us arguing over whose turn it was to do the dishes and clean up.

The houses in Auchenflower were literally two metres apart, and the group of single working-class girls next door would yell at us through the window and tempt us to go over. Brett ended up moving into a house with one of them.

In early 1990, when I was starting my second degree at the Queensland University of Technology (QUT), I returned from PNG three weeks late for classes because of a painting contract that I was doing for the Westpac Bank. I attended my first lectures at QUT with paint still stuck in my hair.

I only had a year left to complete this second degree in Banking and Finance, but was so exhausted by living from hand-to-mouth for four years that I went home and did not return. I do regret this and in hindsight, if I had been able to get a bit more financial support at the time, I would have liked to complete the second degree and do an MBA.

When I got home to Alotau, I joined the Certified Practising Accountants of PNG, and over an eighteen-month period, sat for the seven exams for Associate

Membership. I topped five of the seven exams nationally, and the prize was K500 per exam!

I made a calculated decision to return to PNG, foregoing my Australian Permanent Residency, a steady banking job, and my high school sweet-heart, based on my belief of better financial prospects. This was still my fixed mindset. But I also had an underlying sense that my country needed me more than Australia did. It was this calling deep in my heart that proved to be the closer to the truth of me.

At home, I immediately launched into a series of small-scale businesses with the intention to generate cashflow to invest into passive investments and property. I stayed behind Dad's place until I built my first house. As soon as I could, I approached the Bank and began to utilize debt capital. I undertook a series of property developments when interest rates were at a massive 24 percent, and battled my way through, slowly building up equity.

In 1994, three years after leaving Uni, I went to Mendi for two years to run Kiburu Lodge, and then take up a position as Financial Controller for Global Constructions. All the while, I tried to put savings into land and property.

In 1997, I returned to Alotau, and ran Masurina Constructions for several years before becoming a Tax Agent and specializing in tax return preparation and advice. I handled the accounting for the separation of Masurina Limited and Nako Fisheries in 2000, as John Luke Critten and my father separated business ways after 25 years.

In 2004, I went to Lae and spent some time as the financial controller for Mountain Fuel Freighters, Morobe Customs and Cartage, Mountain Transport, and Mountain Property Holdings, on behalf of the Porgera landowners. I worked seven days a week, as the expatriates from Barrick, who ran the Porgera Gold Mine and provided our senior management, were on a fly-in-fly-out arrangement, with two weeks on and two weeks off. They worked 12-hour days because of this and I was not able to rest adequately, as they rotated in and out.

It was extremely stressful, and at one stage, I was handling ten cases of claims at the same time, from landowners on the Highlands Highway for alleged damages caused by our fuel cartage tankers in accidents on the road.

When I had enough in 2006, the Managing Director of the parent company, Ipili Porgera Investments, Don Flanagan, was terminated by the board and incoming Managing Director, Scott O'Reilly, offered to relocate my family to Cairns, put me on the FIFO arrangement, and double my salary. I was already on a significant package in Australian dollars, and this was very tempting indeed. Any sane man would have grabbed it. However, it wasn't the money at this stage. I was just burned out, having put my all into the job.

I went home in 2006, built Chascorp Haus in the main street of Alotau, and stood for my first election in 2007.

Through a combination of factors, I am a relatively wealthy man now, and don't have to work for money anymore. I would have been much wealthier though, if I did not spend the last fifteen years in politics. I am richer in greater ways though, from this experience, including in realizing that my real calling and interest is more in tune with the same things my forebears stood for – a conviction in the principles of our Faith, a determination to live out those principles, a commitment to family, and a commitment to a life of service to others.

I was obsessed with making money at the outset, and my university experience exacerbated this. Over time, I grew to realize though that making money is definitely not my passion. I also realize that those who make real wealth are those who are passionate about creating value, not money. The money comes as a consequence of that value.

When my father, who is the most unlikely business man you'll ever find, spent years building the Masurina business, and painfully helping the landowners to develop the KB Development subdivision, and the Toudikwa subdivision, he was not thinking about money. He was concerned about how to empower the landowners. He was concerned about the expansion of the town. He was concerned about the land being lost because of squatter encroachment and informal development.

The subsequent result, years later, was the generation of hundreds of millions of Kina through the formalization of the land. The beneficiaries are in the thousands of people. Apart from the landowners, and the church, there are many, many new homeowners who have been able to utilize proper titles and get loans from the bank. The town is able to expand in an organized and formal way and the province is able to benefit from a properly functioning town.

Wealth is created through good ideas, driven by a desire to help others honestly through goods and services. Because you are passionate about the idea, you work at it, exercising your discipline and knowledge, and the blessings and rewards flow towards you as a consequence.

The pursuit of money for its own sake will not bring satisfaction beyond a certain point. And if your focus is on money and material things, you will neglect the things that are of a value that is not quantifiable in monetary terms. These are the intimate and not so intimate relationships that you build over a lifetime based on love and trust.

Making money is a subset of the bigger imperative that you are sufficiently organized to be financially independent and hopefully, eventually in a position to be a net contributor rather than a burden. Everyone has to add value in one way or the other, not consume value, be it financial or otherwise.

There are certain factors which you should develop in order to best position yourself to add value to what you generate and how you attract wealth, but these are things that are almost universal to everything you need to do anyway. There are also the basic principles of business and capital growth to understand.

You are required to skill and educate yourself as best you can, given your circumstances. You need to think strategically ahead to choose the best path, given your interests. You need to work hard and consistently, with discipline at what you choose to do. You need to think about how to provide a genuine need for others. You need to begin the process of capital accumulation as soon as possible. The number one literal factor in wealth generation is time, compound interest, and capital gains.

But always remember that the physical journey and our physical cravings are a passage on the continuum to proximity to The Lord. The better we are able to discipline ourselves to a mental and spiritual transcendence over the physical self, and genuinely attempt to adhere to actions out of love and service, the more we attract the abundance of the universe including material wealth, but then, paradoxically, the less important these material things become to you.

Jeffrey, Owen, and Charles K. Abel, January 1997.

Charles K. Abel, painting contract to pay for uni, 1987.

Chapter 10

Running for No Reason

On the 14th of September 2018, I boarded an Air Niugini flight from Nandi to Port Moresby, via Honiara. I had just completed an eight day, around the world promotion of our country's first-ever sovereign bond. As the plane ascended into the Pacific sky, I began to experience a shortness of breath. It felt like there was no air in the plane. I had to struggle to keep conscious. I realized that I had an issue with my heart that could not be ignored any longer. The stress of work, lack of sleep, and my strict training program had caught up with me. I had always thought that I was immortal. I was one of the hardest working Members of Parliament and probably the fittest. As I lay naked on the operating theatre in Raffles Hospital Singapore, and wires were inserted into my heart through the artery in my leg, I understood that I had pushed myself too far.

Arnold Schwarzenegger once said that looking good was feeling good! There are many valuable things to learn from this amazing man who emigrated to the United States in 1968 with hardly a word of English, with his good buddy and training partner Franco Columbo. One of his many legacies was the huge role he played in the promotion of bodybuilding and fitness.

Back in Arnold's day, and even at my introduction to the gym and weight training in 1983 as a 15-year-old (same time that Arnold started training), 'pumping iron' and 'bodybuilding' were definitely seen as a fringe sport undertaken by 'steroid heads' who performed strange rituals in dingy basements.

Today, it is a fundamental part of the training regimen of nearly every physical sport. There are gyms everywhere, and the fitness and lifestyle industries are worth hundreds of billions of dollars worldwide. Open social media platforms such as Youtube, and you get the impression that everyone is hitting the gym these days.

I remember in the late 1970s watching Dad play rugby league in the local competition. He stood out like a sore thumb, being the only white man on the field most times, but also being a 'ranga' or redhead with his flowing red hair and headband. The players would huddle in at halftime and we juniors would struggle and stretch to get our heads in and listen to the breakdown. It seemed to me that the priority was always a 'chew' (betelnut) and a cigarette! These were vital necessities before any possibility of further play.

In those days nearly every one smoked. If you boarded a flight to Port Moresby you would disembark totally stinking of cigarette smoke because everyone onboard had been smoking. No-one blinked an eye (except to see through the fog of smoke). It was the done thing. Every seat on the plane had an ashtray built into the arm rest stuffed full of cigarette butts. We were all smokers back then, actively or passively. You literally had no choice.

Dad loved sports, and notwithstanding the smoking and drinking, we grew up with a Dad who was always active right up to his tennis playing into his early 80s. I can remember going running with him to the gravel pit and back regularly, a four kilometre run, and how people would stare at us because it was so unusual to see people ***running for no reason***, especially in the rugby off season.

I started training in 1983 while in Grade 9, at Bruce Dunn's Maroochydore Gym on Wises Road, Maroochydore, Sunshine Coast, Queensland. My chiropractor said that I had a lifted tendon in my right knee from playing soccer and a growth spurt (I was in the Queensland Churches Schoolboy soccer team), and needed some resistance exercises to build back wasted muscle. We were living with my Grandma and Aunty Liz (Elizabeth Abel) at the time, on Bronzewing Avenue, Buderim. Aunty Liz sewed me some sandbags using the powdered white sand from the beaches of the Sunshine Coast, to do leg extensions, and rebuild my leg muscles.

By the way, the Sunshine Coast has some of the best beaches and surf in the world. I got my first surfboard – a single fin Mactavish from an old 'skeg' next door, in 1982, and began a love affair with surfing that is another story. The Sunshine Coast was a backwater in those days. Today, it rivals the Gold Coast to the south of Brisbane City. Oh, if I had been in a position to buy some real estate back then!

Cecil's son, Andrew Abel, turned up a short time later, after six months in hospital with a badly broken leg, to attend Burnside High School in Nambour. He also caught the surfing bug and to this day champions the development of surf tourism in PNG.

I would faithfully do my leg extensions after school every day until Aunty Liz took me down to meet Bruce Dunn at Maroochydore Gym, and paid for six months membership.

There is no doubt much of what drives me, and probably many of us, is an underlying insecurity about our worth and ability. There is a love of sport and physical activity that is evident throughout our family history, but my deep insecurities, combined with an affinity for discipline and hard work made training, bodybuilding and I a perfect marriage.

Every afternoon, after school, I would ride my bike to the gym which was conveniently located on the way home. My brother, Owen, and I would ride down for a surf every morning before school as well. Buderim is the oldest European settlement on the Sunshine Coast, and 180 metres above sea level. Imagine a downhill ride with surfboard under one arm, negotiating traffic, and often on a cold winter morning. The water was freezing.

Poor Grandma would have to drive down and wave us out of the surf with her hanky so we could get to school on time. We would strap our boards on the car roof rack and ride back up the hill to Buderim from Alexandra Headlands. The ride down was always easier.

The gym became a ritual, almost religious. A tribe, collectively suffering at the rack. Of course, the ignorant public did not understand. How could they? The curls, deadlifts, chins, squats, and bench. It was 'no pain no gain'. And as I saw the gains, got the compliments, I was spurred deeper into the abyss.

Mr. Australia and Mr. Queensland also trained at the Maroochydore Gym. I eventually became the training partner for Mr. Queensland - Middleweight. These guys were hardcore, and on the 'juice' (anabolic steroids). They were super strong. We were doing weighted pull ups, weighted dips and heavy squatting and bench press. I remember doing five plated squats for reps (220kg) one day. I couldn't see out of one eye after the set and looked in the mirror. I had burst a blood vessel in the eye.

Bruce Dunn worked hard on building gym membership with aerobics and dance classes, as well, in an adjacent room. It was the days of 'breakdancing', which was the rage, but it never caught on with me. I was with the long-term dance – basic fitness and lifting.

Bruce mentioned to me one day, in early 1985, that some of the guys were going to compete in the upcoming NPC International Federation of Body Building Gold Coast and Queensland Bodybuilding Championships, which were two separate events. He asked if I wanted to have a go. I'd only being training for a year and a half. It still seemed weird to me, shaving down, oiling up and striking poses in your underwear. I did it of course! I was bronzed with a sun-bleached afro from surfing, sixteen years old and came third in the Gold Coast Coast Bodybuilding Championships 1985 Teenage Division, and come second in the Queensland Bodybuilding Championships Teenage Division on the Gold Coast later that year. These days you have to be at least eighteen years of age to compete in any division.

It was all part of my high school experience. I tried nearly everything. The thing that was the toughest about competing was the dieting, not the training. You had to hit the stage beefed up and ripped. When you are a growing teenager, surfing every day, lifting weights in the afternoon, you are literally starving all the time anyway.

The University of Queensland (UQ), St. Lucia Campus has a magnificent location on the bend of the Brisbane River. It has all kinds of sporting facilities, including a wonderful gym. I was lucky enough to attend UQ from 1987 to 1989 to complete a Bachelor of Economics degree, and the gym was my second home, but in more ways than one.

In my second year, Dad decided it was time to stop supporting my brother and I, and we had to work a variety of casual jobs, including in my case, bouncer work at different nightclubs, waitering, and house painting for my best friend Tim Johnson's father's business.

The main work I did in my second year though was gym coaching for ten dollars an hour at the UQ gym. I would often miss classes for the convenience of clients, and sometimes do up to eight sessions a day. My voice would be hoarse from non-stop talking – a trait that continues to annoy people to this day. This work came to an abrupt halt when the University Sports Science Faculty decided it was inappropriate to have non-faculty students coaching gym classes. They thought it was better for those with more technical knowledge of movement science to teach people how to lift weights, even though they themselves had not touched a dumbbell in their lives. Obviously, those of us, now unemployed, were not impressed!

Some 39 years later, I still train almost every day and you can see some of this on my social media.

I've always used some combination of resistance training (lifting heavy objects up and putting them down), and cardiovascular training (repetitious stuff that makes you puff, like running, burpees, or skipping). The objective is to have fun and look and feel your best, and I believe there are deeper justifications to be tapped into as well.

My great grandfather believed that sport was an integral part of a holistic life and took great pride in the exploits of the Kwato cricket team. My father continued to exercise right up until the end. He was lean and fit his whole life.

I return to the theme of a 'code of conduct' founded in Faith and emanating in love and responsible actions towards ourselves and others. This encompasses discipline and restraint in how you treat your body, including the urge to gluttony (overeating) and sloth (laziness).

In the early days I just followed the standard three day split of weight training – LEGS, PUSH (chest, shoulders, triceps), PULL (back, biceps, traps, forearms). I lifted as heavy as possible in every workout! Because we were constantly surfing, playing soccer, rugby, and basketball we stayed lean as well.

Of course, you get older, married, lose motivation, and the stomach starts to poke out, the butt recedes and the legs get skinnier! It's harder to keep that body moving.

You don't have to be mad like me and train every day at 54 years of age, but I can recommend that you dedicate at least three days a week to some exercise. The hardest part is the beginning. After that you can't stop! It's so uplifting – sorry about the pun.

At the moment, I do a two-day split - a full body, weights workout day, then a cardio day, on rotation. I will rest one day per week. On the weights day I will usually do one compound movement for lower body (such as squats, deadlifts, walking lunges) and one compound movement for upper body (such as bench press, bent rows). This is apart from training all muscle groups separately as well – glutes, hamstrings, calves, quads, chest, back, traps, shoulders, biceps, triceps, forearms, and neck. I will always start with a weaker developed body part.

On the cardio day, I will do 45 minutes of steady state cardio (occasionally I will throw in some more high intensity sprints or high jumps when the steady state, low intensity gets too boring), volume work on abdominals and then a full body stretch.

After six weeks, I will vary the split depending on how my body is reacting. My current one meal a day and cardio every second day has meant I've dropped too much muscle so I will move to a three-day split with an upper body weights day, lower body day, and cardio day. Instead of one meal a day I will add a second meal. Then see how that goes for six weeks.

Muscles need a combination of heavy weight stress and volume training. Heavy is for size, and volume for hardness and quality. In each case, there must be a level of intensity and failure or exhaustion of the muscle in order to induce a response from the body. If you don't stress the muscle, it will not adapt to the applied stress.

You then need to feed the muscles the necessary calories and nutrients. Down-load (less than maximum weight) days and rest days are important as is variety of exercise. If your main goal is to build muscle, there is no getting away from the basic compound movements with a repetition range of five to fifteen. This means heavy squats, deadlifts, bent rows, and bench press.

In order to lose weight, you need to be in a calorie deficit. The number of calories you are putting in your mouth must be less than the calories you are burning through Non-Exercise Activity Thermogenesis (the energy you are burning by just being alive and moving around), and exercise. These are the immutable laws of thermodynamics.

In order to gain or maintain muscle and lose fat, you need a combination of both resistance training and resistance dieting!

In the case of abdominals ('six pack'), it is better to emphasize volume, core and vacuum style exercises to keep the waist trim and tight. If the abdominals are trained in the same way that other muscle groups are trained it may lead to larger bulkier abdominals and because we tend to carry more fat on the waist it just gives a thicker appearance to the waist. Rather, you want larger shoulders and a narrower waist.

Training abdominals will not make you lose fat around the waist. Reducing what you eat and doing more intensive exercise movements, particularly of a cardiovascular nature over a sustained period, will do that.

Stretching reduces the risk of injury and helps you to better perform movements mechanically, and apply stress to the muscle, rather than the tendons or joints. Stretching prolongs your ability to perform movements as you age.

As I have aged, I have peaked out in terms of a weight lifting ceiling, although I can still squat 4.5 plates (200 kg) at 54 years old for example, but have compensated for this with volume and intensity techniques. Such is my love, or addiction, to weight training, I will train whether I am in a remote village or on a boat using bands or bodyweight.

Much of the time I train alone, but this is only because of lack of access to a public gym. When I occasionally get access to a good public gym, it's like I'm in a theme park with more rides than I know what to do with. Having a training partner means you can lift heavier because he or she can 'spot' you and it can motivate you generally as well. To train alone over a period of time takes mental fortitude.

The physicality, stress, and pain of the exertion brings me to the moment. It calms my inner quarreling, and takes me away from my conscious mind. It is a form of meditation. Perhaps it's just self-flagellation to ease a conscience!

I have experimented with all types of dieting and fasting variations. I have measured my calorie intake to determine my base metabolic sustenance calorie intake, and varied intake around it to maintain periodic calorie deficit states to try and maintain a body fat percentage at around ten to fifteen percent.

The idea is to maximize lean muscle mass and minimize fat retention. The training regime of weights and cardio have obvious health enhancing outcomes of cardio-vascular health and muscle and bone retention and strength. The dieting maintains a healthy body weight and dietary input on macro-nutrient and micro-nutrient levels.

The extent that many of us are going to these days, including me, does go beyond what is required from a purely health perspective. It becomes a cosmetic and perhaps vain-glorious pursuit, and can even be detrimental to health. Once body fat goes below a certain point or performance enhancing drugs are used, then this can be so. It is only a small percentage of people who have the necessary discipline or motivation to go to this extent though. The vast majority of people in the first world or those in lesser developed countries who have access to food are overweight and don't exercise enough. The leading cause of death in the United States is heart disease. In Papua New Guinea, lifestyle diseases are a relatively new and growing cause of health issues. As the country develops, tuberculosis and malaria are being replaced by strokes, diabetes, and heart disease.

Currently, I eat only one meal a day and have been doing that for more than a year. I eat within a window of four hours between 12-midday to 4p.m. I eat to satiety and without restriction, except that I make the bulk of the meal protein-based and I eat the protein portion first. Protein at a minimum of one gram per day per pound of body weight is required to sustain muscle growth and protein is also more satiating or filling than carbohydrates. I take a multivitamin, magnesium, calcium, and Omega-3 (fish oil) as dietary supplements.

There are positive benefits to fasting when your body is given time to focus on repair and maintenance without the constant distraction of having to process and absorb large amounts of food.

Diet is the primary determinant of your metabolic health. Overly processed foods and refined sugar are the killers. Whole foods are the way to go, and realize that human beings are naturally meat eaters.

In the natural historic state, *homo sapiens* and their predecessors did not eat three large meals a day, but rather, grazed when they could and had the occasional large protein meal after a kill. There were often periods of famine. This necessitated the need to be able to store calories in the form of fat and always keep a certain level of fat ready for the next famine. When we travel below this level, as a result of external circumstances such as famine or self-induced calorie restrictions, the body will tap into the fat reserves and even begin to break down muscles to access energy. Through a combination of resistance training, and a protein emphasized diet with an overall calorie deficit, you can body 'recomposition' to reduce fat and increase muscle. This calorie deficit state can only be sustained for temporary periods. A bodybuilder will push to extremely low body fat levels for a show but return to more normal levels, post-show.

The objective is to reach and maintain a good level of muscle, health fat levels, and feel and look your best.

Sleep and managing your stress levels are very important as I discovered only too well when my heart started playing up. I've always struggled with my sleep, as discussed in another chapter. One simple yet helpful pointer here is to not drink coffee in the afternoon onwards until bedtime. If you drink strong coffee, as I do, it can remain in your system for up to eight hours and definitely affect your sleep.

Taking charge of your body and health through self-discipline, sacrifice, and hard work, is a prerequisite in a life of meaning and value. Everything starts with you taking responsibility for the things you can control. At the risk of repeating an old adage; "your body is a temple, a gift from God, a blessing, the vessel through which you love and live in this phase of the journey."

Charles K. Abel, Alotau, 9th February 2019

Cricket in the early 1900s, Kwato Island.

National Softball Championships, Lae, 1994.

Alotau Rugby League Grandfinal, 1994.

National Basketball Championships, Port Moresby, 2018.

Chapter 11

Coconut Ukulele

We huddled back stage in absolute terror. There was a massive crowd of at least five thousand people outside, and they were in a demanding mood. To us small town boys it seemed like ten thousand. We had only ever played in front of small crowds and bush discos before. This was 1999 in the big smoke, Port Moresby City, and the famous Port Moresby Show.

A couple of the bands before us had been booed off the stage. I could hear as the crowd even threw empty bottles on the stage as one group took too long to tune up.

The solo artists who simply used the professional CHM Super Sound stage band, with the famous sound engineers and guitarists, Lister Laka, Dika Dai, and George Luff had it much easier.

We were a full live band unit, but without the polish and experience of the Moresby bands, or the brilliant Super Sound band.

There was Panu Elijah on lead guitar, Franklin Evi on drums, Richard Gelu on rhythm guitar, Phillip Kari on bass, and Phillip Falaniki from the Solomon Islands on the keys.

We were unbelievably nervous and basically chain-smoking as we listened to the carnage on stage.

I called the boys together and tried to put on a brave face. "Boys, no fuck around tuning up on stage, number one. Number two, whatever mistake you make just keep going, do not stop. We have done this many times, just a bigger crowd, that's all. We got this."

As I charged on stage I knew as always that the band would feed off my energy in front. If I was fired up and having a good time the music came free and naturally from the boys. We had to kill the first number as this was a tough crowd, and I sang an original from the new album called *Sagarai Girl*, a reggae/rock number, written by Frankie. The crowd had never heard these songs before or the Wabo Knights band. They had not seen a lead singer run around the stage like me. They loved it and after the second song they wanted a third. We smashed it.

We were in town as the Wabo Knights to record our first album with the Chin H Meen recording studios, with engineer Eddie Elias. The studio asked us to do a live audition. We ate it up as we were a live band at heart, and I was the 'live wire' front man. When it came to the recording process though, we did not have a clue. Eddie kept asking me to stop moving around and doing strange things with my voice.

The studio was sufficiently impressed and asked us to play at the annual Port Moresby Show that was on at that time.

When I returned from Mendi in the Southern Highlands in 1996, I ran Masurina Constructions for a time, and some of the local boys would come and practise their guitars and bang on improvised drums on our side of the duplex in which we were living. We had grown up in small town Alotau so retained connections with school mates, nephews, and the local villagers.

We had been around music all our lives. Dad always had a guitar in the house and would pick it up and smash out some of the ancient songs that he knew.

As I listened to all his plastic records after school, I developed a love and appreciation for the Beatles, Credence Clearwater Revival, The Seekers, The Doobie Brothers, Elton John, and The Rolling Stones.

When we were in primary school, Dad actually made **ukuleles** for us out of timber and **coconut**. He glued a shaped piece of hardwood over the dried hull of a coconut to provide the neck and body. He then drilled holes at the end of the arm and inserted wooden keys which tightened fishing line strings. We had lessons in ukulele chords and songs after that.

Mrs. Jacki George was my English teacher, and my guitar teacher. She called me into her office one day and said, "I want to ask you something." My first thought was, - 'uh oh'.

I was in Grade 9 at Immanuel Lutheran College on the Sunshine Coast, Australia. Mrs. George was a really likeable and understanding teacher and she knew that I would find it hard to refuse a request from her.

"Charlie, how's guitar practice going?"

"All good Mrs. George, thank you."

"How would you like to be in a school gospel band?"

I knew Jackie and her husband Barry were into folk music and had their own band. They had a cool hippie vibe about them.

I just knew though that a gospel band would not go down well with some of my mates. In high school I would cop so much shit over it. I hesitated and tried to formulate a no answer in a very polite manner. Before I could say anything, she said. "Justin (Wilkie) and Scott (Chapman) have signed up already. So have Bronwyn (Shultz) and Inge (Hall). The band is called Hosanna."

"How am I going to get out of this?" I thought. Hosanna is really gay sounding as well.

Sounding as interested as I could, I replied, "Sounds really good, let me talk to Justin about it."

Hosanna went on to be quite a feature at different festivals all around the Sunshine Coast. We played at numerous concerts at school and school assemblies. I learned a lot about stage presence, harmonies, and getting on in a band.

And yes, I did cop a lot of shit from my surfing and bodybuilding mates.

As the boys came to the house for 'practice', I would join them, and before long my obsessive, compulsive tendencies began to hum and, began a journey Hacy would speak less favourably about – the Wabo Knights journey.

It literally becomes an obsession almost to the exclusion of everything else. The endless practising, smashing bottles when the boys would drink during practice, arguments with Hacy when I would neglect my family duties, and long nights at the studio.

There was no money to be made out of it whatsoever. The benefit was always weighted in favour of the studio. The artist got very little for their creative input. I would also say that the hours put in by the studio engineers was not properly recognized. It was just passion and infatuation. We wrote our own songs and played them live everywhere.

From the early days, we had Panu Elijah on lead guitar and vocals, Frankie Evi on the drums, Phillip Kari on bass, Ritchie Gelu on rhythm guitar and Philip Falaniki on the keys. I was the front man. Others would come and go, and sub in and out.

On many occasions we would play as a three-piece band with two guitars and drums only. I would take the drums and sing. I can remember nights at the Cameron Club where the band was on the same floor level as the crowd. We would have the crowd crush in on us. I would have a beer and cigarette on the floor, be playing the drums and singing, leaning over to pick up the hihat as it was knocked over by someone while continuing to play and sing. Take a swig of beer and a puff on the cigarette, wipe the sweat out of my eyes and play another song. We took every opportunity to play. By the time the song, Wabo, became a hit off the first album and we were invited to Moresby we were quite a polished stage band and I could play the stage and the crowd.

We recorded three studio albums and had two national Number One hits on the CHM Video Countdown – Wabo and One Pis Mangi, and several other hits such as Sagarai Girl, Lucky Bump, and Ata Ina. The videos from the first two songs made me quite famous nationally. I was signing autographs and getting a big head.

One of the things I am most proud of was leading somewhat of a revival in the Milne Bay music and recording scene. A number of bands rose out of this era including the Corner Joins, Mid Street Band, and the 28 Band.

Three members of the Wabo Knights went on to do solo albums and enjoy success in their own right.

I rubbed shoulders with some great musicians like Oshen, Moses Tau, Lister and Amon Serum, Hitsy Golou, John Faunt, George Luff, Lister Laka, Wamsi Ilau, Steve Lahui, and Dika Dai.

I met with Mr. Raymond Chin of Chin Hoi Min Studios to talk about artists royalties and how to boost sales.

My popularity through music helped me win my first election in 2007. I would use the band in all my election campaigns and sing some songs to fire up the crowd before playing the politics!

My younger brother, Owen, has initiated the annual music festival - 'Out Loud', which grows in popularity every year.

Charles K. Abel, 1999

Wabo Knights, Volume 2, 2002

Port Moresby Show, June 1999.

Chapter 12

Another Planet

It was another busy and raucous night at Kiburu Lodge outside of Mendi Town in the Southern Highlands of Papua New Guinea.

Kiburu Lodge is located on the banks of the Mendi River, with beautiful bungalows made from local timbers, cane, and kunai grass thatched roofs. The main restaurant and reception with the old furnace in the middle of the lounge and balcony overlooking the river was something reminiscent of an old Kenyan hunting lodge, where we would gather for warmth as the mist rolled into the Mendi Valley and the rain drizzled down of an evening.

This lodge was designed for well-to-do tourists from overseas with a mind to bird watching or trout fishing in their safari suits and with cameras and binoculars. It was they who were meant to sit around the furnace, quietly sipping their wine and coffee, and discussing the vagaries of bird species and the different headdresses displayed at the cultural 'singsing'.

The scene on this night and every night rather, was that of local tourists, townsfolk, and highway men mingling in various states of inebriation out in the makeshift 'boybar' or in the lounge. Their muddy boots, bearded faces and boisterous tones clashed with the backdrop.

All was good as far as my bosses were concerned. If we couldn't make enough money from selling beds and bird watching, we would make it through a roaring restaurant trade with a very liquid diet.

This was 1994, and much of the Highlands was under a liquor ban because of the law-and-order issues, particularly following the 1992 National Elections. This meant that alcohol could only be served at licensed restaurants. We were trucking and flying in the SP brand of local beer by the hundreds of cartons a week.

I had recently taken up the job as manager of Kiburu Lodge and soon realized I was in the hotbed of one of the most violent cultures in our country, selling "firewater" by the bucket every night.

I dealt with guns, threats, and fights on a nightly basis. It was not the job that I had signed up for. But, as usual, I took it head on.

On the night in question, gunfire suddenly broke the air outside and one of the security guards burst into the kitchen where I was talking to the staff and said, "Bos, man ya belhat na kam!" (Boss he is angry and came back). "Husait?" (Who?), I asked. "****!". "Em spaksense pinis" (He is already drunk).

****, an ex-policeman had been our head of security. I had sacked him for drinking on duty.

"Orait, bai mi kam" (I'll come out), I said wearily. It never stopped.

As I stepped out onto the karanas graveled car park I had one guard with me, Peter. The moon was out and I could see a small group of men standing with **** who was in front with a handgun in his hand, hanging by his side. This must have been the source of the gunfire.

"****, gutla yu kam bek lo monin time, yu wok lo phretim ol man natin." (****, its best you come back in the morning, you are scaring everybody), I said.

He was very drunk and obviously upset, "Bai mi sutim yu, harim!" was his response. "Mi no pikinini blo yu!" (I will shoot you, you hear, I'm not your child).

As he spoke, he moved towards me and raised the gun. Peter stepped between us. I saw a police mobile squad landcruiser drive in to the carpark, perhaps alerted by the gunshots. One of the mob reached over and grabbed Peter by the shirt. Peter immediately punched him in the face. There was a drizzle and I saw his fist slide across the wet face and it cut open and the blood spurted. A scuffle broke out. I was completely sober and ducking and weaving as they came at me. The mobile squad let off a fusillade of automatic gunfire into the sky and everyone ran for their lives. My shirt was torn and chest scratched but I was ok. Peter's face was bleeding.

The next morning, I took the short walk from the manager's house back to the Lodge. It is actually a beautiful part of the world, crisp and cool, rolling hills and freezing, tumbling rivers. The people are full of character, strong willed, and renowned for their aggressive ways. I was slowly earning the local people's respect by just being firm and fair at all times. This was to be another day in the 'getting to know each other' process, as I soon discovered.

There was absolutely no-one around when I got to the Lodge. I saw Peter with a big bandage around his head, sitting by himself in the carpark.

"Peter, olgeta man meri we?" (Where is everybody?), I asked him.

"Bos ol ronwei", (they ran away) he said. "Bos, line ya, ol bum na weitim yumi antap lo maket" (the people have gathered and are waiting for us at the market), Peter said.

"Blo wanem?" (What for?)

"Ol belhat na stap" (They are angry and waiting)

"Oiyo pilisi, Mendi! Ok yumi go" (Oh Mendi! Ok let's go)

We both climbed into the lodge bus. Good old Eric Pape, one of the senior staff, had emerged and said he would drive us.

When we arrived at the market, I could see the usual vendors had cleared the area and there were two truckloads of people. They had painted their faces black and were all fully armed with machetes, axes and bows and arrows. I thought – Lord, what am I even doing in this place!??

I steeled myself and as I stepped out of the bus, I was assailed by the screeching of women folk and the yelling and brandishing from the trucks.

"Yu katim pikinini blo mipla blo wanem!? Yu wanem kain man!? Bai yu mekim wanem now!?" (You have cut our child for no reason, what sort of person are you? What are you going to do now?)

There was a boy standing before them with a large cut down his face. The atmosphere was so tense. I had to be brave and place my words carefully. I was not ready to die yet!

"Pastime mi tok sore steret lo bagarap pikinini boi bin kissim. Lon aste nite yupla kam kirapim hevi lon ples blo Francis Awesa yet. Mi wok man sol blo em. Mi lukautim kampani blo em. Nau hevi kamap, boi ya kisim bagarap, na tu yu lukim face blo Pita. Em kisim bikpla bagarap wantaim. Sapos yu laikim kompensason, tu yu mas mekim lo Pita wankain."

(Firstly, I am very sorry for what has happened to the boy. You came last night and made trouble at the place of Francis Awesa (the chief and main owner of Kiburu Lodge). I just work for him only. I look after his company. A problem has come up now but look at the face of Peter. He also has been beaten up. If you want compensation, you must also compensate Peter.)

It seemed to quiet them, and after an awkward moment I slowly retreated back to the bus and we drove down to the Lodge again.

"Boss, you said the right thing," was Eric's only comment.

It was the Sir Danny Leahy Oval in Goroka, the crowd was churning in a frenzy. The Mendi Muruks were playing the Goroka Lahanis in the rugby league preliminary final of the Inter-City Cup – the national competition.

I was seated on the side-line with the Muruks team, Hacy was with me. I watched in astonishment as a member of the Lahanis bench stepped onto the field and tripped the Muruks winger over. I looked to the linesman who ignored the incident, the referee, who was an Australian, was distracted. The crowd roared. I stood up with my hands raised in protest. As I did so I turned in time to see a local lad run up behind me from the crowd with a large rock in his right hand. He made to throw it at me and as I turned and winced, he dropped the rock.

I felt the sky crushing in on me. The alarm bells were going off in my head. Why did I bring Hacy? She had insisted on coming. I tried to explain to her the nature of rugby in the Highlands. It was too late now. I had to think on my feet. The Muruks had a two-point lead and it was almost half time. I calmed myself and waited. As the half time hooter sounded, I rose slowly and tapped Hacy on the shoulder. "We are leaving."

Wesley Pape, the big bearded Kiburu man, looked at me and nodded gently. His eyes told me everything.

We made our way past the teeming crowd towards the exit. They were screaming and swearing at me, telling me to go back. As I got to the gate I could hear them yelling, "Noken opim gate, noken opim!!" (don't open the gate)

Wesley grabbed the attendant by the neck and said firmly, "F...n opim gate, nau tasol." (Open the gate now) I realized later that they only opened the gate because Wesley was known to them as a feared rugby legend of years past, playing for Mendi and Goroka as well.

We scurried out of the reluctantly opened gate and made our way back to the Bird of Paradise Hotel in our hired Toyota 10-seater. "Wes, we have to get out of this Town.", I said.

"Boss yumi weitim tutark." (We wait for nightfall.)

We waited nervously at the Hotel, worried about the players and management still at the field.

Within twenty minutes there was the burst of gunfire, yelling, and screaming. People were running in the streets. I could smell the teargas. Some years ago, I had been involved in trying to control a large fight. As I held on to two of the culprits around their necks, one of them had me by the balls. It was a stalemate, I was strong as an ox and was going to rip his head off, or lose my ball sack.

The police who had arrived on the scene shot a canister of teargas at us and it bounced off the wall and erupted right into our faces. It was like somebody had put a blowtorch on my eyeballs. I dropped everything and staggered away holding my face and slipping and sliding on broken glass in my thongs.

I will never forget the smell and taste of teargas. I could smell it now in the streets of Goroka Town.

We could only lock ourselves in the room and wait it out.

Eventually, there were sirens and the contingent of police who had escorted us from Mendi arrived with the team. They were a mess. Robert Posu, the team manager had been rushed to hospital with a fractured skull and most of the team were bleeding and bruised.

The police cordoned off the hotel and at 11 p.m. that night we were escorted out of Goroka in a convoy. I did not feel safe until we were past the Southern Highlands border and 'home' again.

Kiburu Lodge were major sponsors of the Mendi Muruks and I got to know many of their great players. Legends like Raymond Karl from Ialibu would come and stay at my little cottage. Nande Yer, Rueben Ruing, Cedrick Kengi, Petrus Thomas (later to join me in Parliament), and Samuel Pinpin would go on to play for the Kumuls. Samuel Pinpin presented me with his Kumul jersey on his first selection on the bench.

I spent six months running the beautiful Kiburu Lodge before moving into the main office for Global Constructions Limited. Mick Jepson from Pangia Constructions, together with Francis Awesa, the owner of Kiburu Lodge, Bill Howe, and Tim Johnson, the Managing Director and Financial Controller of Iagifu Oil and Gas (landowner company at the Kutubu Oil fields), and Sosoro Hewago, a landowner from Kutubu, had purchased the Mendi branch of Pangia Constructions to form the ambitiously named 'Global Constructions'. It was primarily a roadworks company, accessing maintenance contracts with the Department of Works. It had also leased Kiburu Lodge from Francis Awesa, who wasn't particularly impressed with the beer selling side of things.

I became the financial controller for Global Constructions, and gave it my all, working long hours and punishing my little family. Mick Jepson was 'ex-Special Air Services' in the British Army and claimed he had operated as a sniper. He was my boss, brilliant, rough as they come and only interested in money and drinking. One day we were sitting in the office and Mick drove in. It wasn't long before one of the locals rushed in with a Tramontina long-bladed bush knife. He was livid about something and in a terrible rage. As he rushed into the office, Mick drew his revolver, stood up suddenly and grabbed the man by the head before he knew what was happening. He jammed the gun in his mouth hard and said very slowly and firmly, "I will f..in kill you right now," in his thick Derbyshire accent.

The man dropped his knife and retreated with blood coming from his mouth.

I watched Mick one night when we had a big fight going on in the Lodge. He strode in, grabbed a wooden baton from one of the security guards and started jabbing and poking people on their thighs and stomachs. They just collapsed left, right, and centre. One brave man charged him and Mick just pinned his throat against the wall with the baton until he fainted. It was thanks for coming folks and good night at that point.

One morning, I was sitting with Francis Awesa in my office and one of the male grounds man came up hollering about his pay not being right. He did not realize Francis was in my office.

"Yu wanem kin, giaman masta, bai mi reipim meri blo yu!" he screamed through my window. (You fake white man, I will rape your wife).

Francis calmly walked out onto the verandah and punched him in the head. Once the man fell over, he proceeded to stamp on his head with the heel of his shoe. There was blood everywhere before I could stop him.

Francis proceeded to lay down the law, Highland's style,

"Yupla harim gut toktok blo mi. Ol nambis kam lo hia becos mi yet tokim ol lo kam. Em ol wok line blo mi. Sapos you putim liklik finga blo yu antap lo wanpla. Mi bai kilim yu, harim?"

(Listen to me. These (coastal) people are here because I told them to come. They work for me. If you lay one finger on them, I will kill you. Do you hear?).

Francis Awesa would also join me in Parliament in the days ahead. He offered me shares in Global when there was a falling out with the other shareholders. Mick disagreed and offered me more money instead. I was exhausted and chose to go home. Global would continue to grow into one of the biggest constructions companies in the country. Mick Jepson eventually bought Francis out.

I became fluent in Tok Pisin and got to know a beautiful part of our country, and a tough but proud people full of character, in the Highlands. It was almost like **another planet.**

**The Suau language dictionary published in
2013 by Sir Chris Abel.**

Hacy Abel and Charles K. Abel. 1996.

Chapter 13

A Trucking Life

We were several metres up in the air in the cabin of a Kenworth prime mover, with some 40 000 litres of diesel attached in a tanker behind us.

The driver, through tired eyes and a snow speckled beard, took one grease-stained hand off the steering wheel to drop the 18-shift gear down a couple of levels.

"Boss, tyre bruk." He grunted, matter of factly.

We were on the Leron Plains in 2004, heading up the Highlands Highway. It was still in darkness, before sunrise.

As the financial controller of Mountain Fuel Freighters (MFF), I knew pretty much everything you could theoretically know about a highway truck. The mathematical formula we used to calculate the cartage rate per litre for delivering fuel to the Porgera Gold Mine, required intimate costing knowledge of tyres, parts, fuel consumption, and driver performance against different configurations to reach Hagen, then Porgera.

I had spent hours calculating the benefits of establishing a base in Hagen and doing a Lae - Hagen cycle, and Hagen - Porgera cycle, rather than driving one long trip from Lae to Porgera and back. Driver fatigue and accidents were major issues. This was significantly reduced in a double cycle configuration. There came with it the additional costs of an extra base and workshop in Hagen. However, the net savings proved to be significant and the establishment of the Hagen yard and driver accommodation was a significant achievement in my time. The drivers appreciated this.

They worked long and dangerous hours, but were very well paid. Their presence up and down the highway, long hours, and full pockets often led to second and third families along the way, and many unhappy wives.

Shortening the drive by breaking up the transport cycle meant that the drivers were home earlier and more often. This greatly helped family stability. The drivers were also better rested, and did not have to spend so much time dealing with rest houses and extra families along the highway.

I would go out in the mornings, climb on top of the trucks and take dip readings of the fuel tanks myself before they left, to try to work out how fuel was being stolen or siphoned out of the tanks around the special seals that we had on each fuel outlet.

It was amazing the lengths that people went to, to steal diesel, and the creativity of various methods. I would calculate the missing litres, take into account variations due to temperature changes from the coast to the Highlands, and scratch my head as to how it was being stolen.

This time I wanted to actually travel with the truck and driver to experience the trip, first hand, in a prime mover cabin. I had become obsessed with everything to do with the tough business of running a transport business on the Highlands Highway. This was the *trucking life*.

As we climbed down to the asphalt in the pitch darkness, my first thought was security, or the lack of it. We had no escort truck, no crew boy, and no weapons. It was the driver and I, and 40 000 litres of liquid gold.

I was constantly in court with issues of compensation and/or fuel theft on the highway. Diesel is a precious commodity to nearly everyone on this road. When there was a mechanical breakdown near any significant population centre or village, the driver would often be chased away and the tanker looted.

If there was an accident because of brake failure, wet road, or driver fatigue, we would be hit with a myriad of compensation demands for the damage to gardens and waterways from the leaked fuel. In one instance, a tyre had come free, and crashed through village houses, killing someone. At one stage, I literally had ten court cases running at the same time.

To change the tyre, we had to remove the flat and insert a new tyre weighting at least 70-80 kg. We had to place the torch in various positions so we could manoeuvre the tyre together as it was beyond one man. I kept looking over my shoulder the whole time expecting to see some unwelcome visitors.

When we climbed back into the cabin, sweaty and dusty, I was confounded as to how we had even considered letting drivers go it alone. The rationale was that they would radio the rescue vehicle in such situations, but this could take hours, depending on the location on the highway. We would have to reinsert at least one crew member per truck to support the driver, and keep him company on the road.

The Porgera Gold Mine, which was operated by Canadian gold miner, Barrick Niugini Limited, required at least 80 million litres of diesel every year, and it was our job to get six semi-trailers with 40 000 litres in to Porgera every day.

This was a logistical nightmare, to say the least, because of the terrible road conditions, the proximity of the local population to the road in significant numbers, the general lawlessness, and the immense practical value of the product that we were carting.

We were a landowner company, that was established and mentored by the mine, to provide a range of supporting services, including fuel. Ipili Porgera Investments (IPI) was run by a bevy of expatriates, tasked with training the locals, and building business and economic opportunities for the landowners.

I was engaged as the Financial Controller for MFF, and eventually took on all the Lae-based operations including Mountain Transport, Morobe Customs and Cartage, and Mountain Property Holdings. I was paid in Australian dollars like the expatriates, and provided excellent accommodation. By the time I left in 2006, I was offered double my conditions and to be relocated with my family to Cairns, on a fly-in-fly out (FIFO) roster.

The problem, as described previously, was that I was worked like a dog. The expatriates were in and out on a two-week-on, two-week-off roster, but I was permanent. A new team would fly in and work 12-hour days. Then a fresh team would replace them. I was up and down the highway from Lae to the Ten Mile office seven days a week. With my young family it was brutal and I went to work twice with black eyes! Hacy even left me for a while. By the time I was burned out and had given my notice, I was offered FIFO from Cairns. It was too late. I never complained, just worked and worked.

My experience of the expatriate mentors was a positive one on the whole. They earned their money. They drove into us the expectations of international best practice. We had to turn up on time, earn our pay, communicate at all times with our bosses, and run a professional outfit. We made money for our landowners and we were properly paid for it.

The Managing Director for IPI was the eccentric but brilliant Irishman, Don Flanagan. He would spend hours in my office picking my brain. At one point, he grabbed a marking pen and drew all over my office wall. I had to have his hieroglyphics painted over. He was mad, but I learned so much from him.

He finally pushed the local directors too far, and they turfed him out and replaced him with Scott O'Reilly, in what was effectively a coup by Scott.

The multiple benefits of a mine, such as Porgera, need to be seen up close to be fully understood. Obviously, as a country we don't want to rely on mining of minerals or petroleum and gas as a long-term solution. However, to provide the interim jobs, government revenue, a sovereign wealth fund, and economic stimulus towards a more sustainable future, we need some of these projects. I write more in the chapter, **"So Much Gold"**.

The recent events, following the change of government in May of 2019, resulted in the indefinite closure of the Porgera Mine (at the time of writing, April 2023, the Mine is still closed). The Government's reasoning was that the mining lease was expiring and as such the government wanted to renegotiate better terms, including perhaps owning 100 percent of the mine, and Barrick to be paid as merely the operator. Barrick consequently asked to be paid out so they could depart. So began protracted negotiations, with the Government slowly softening its position, over time.

In the meantime, thousands of workers lost their jobs, the Paiam township shut down, hundreds of contractors lost their source of income, many businesses in Lae suffered, and the Government lost hundreds of millions in taxation revenue as the gold price went to historically record levels.

The Enga Provincial Government lost millions in royalties, as did the landowners. Companies such as Ipili Porgera Investments, supplying fuel and catering services to the mine have lost millions of Kina and hundreds of jobs.

The operator of the Porgera Mine had applied years ago for a lease renewal in anticipation of the lease expiry. The Government had been sitting on its hands. When I became Treasurer in 2017, we immediately began negotiations as part of the economic recovery plan (captured in the 100-Day Plan). We asked for some additional free equity and a ten percent production royalty. PNG ended up with 57percent of the net free cashflow, based on these negotiations, **without any additional capital outlay, or the mine having to stop operations.**

The current stalemate and proposed outcome, has not only caused the losses from a mine shut down, but will cost the Government hundreds of millions to buy additional equity, and pay its share of the start-up costs.

There is a certain naivety and lack of commercial experience that we, as a country and a government, take to the negotiating table that wastes so much time and resources. The result is the unnecessary suffering of our people.

I think of all the families that lost their jobs and incomes.

I think of all the additional debt that the government took on because of the continued deficits in our annual budgets partially because of lost opportunities like this.

Mind you, I am talking about past and present governments.

As Planning Minister, I consistently advocated for a proper upgrading of the 800-kilometre Highlands Highway, as the No.1 infrastructure asset of our country, and the lifeline to half our population and numerous resource projects.

When I was Treasurer, we negotiated the multi-tranche Highlands Highway rehabilitation project, for one billion US dollars, from the Asian Development Bank.

I learned so much from my years in Lae, and on the road to Porgera. Sometimes, I think I should have stayed on, taken the big money, and based out of Cairns. I knew in my heart though that home was calling, and I had a few other things to do that were more important than money.

I apologized to my queen, gathered my little family back together, and returned to Alotau. With the money I had saved, which I had invested in Oil Search shares, and made some good capital gains, went to the bank and borrowed to buy land in town and build Chascorp Haus, an office complex. It was 2006, and I mixed cement with the boys in the sun and the rain. My block was right next door to the BSP Bank where, during my Uni days, I got a contract to scrub and paint the bank, and was out on a ladder scrubbing and painting the roof in the eyes of the public.

When I stood for election in 2007, I placed a banner on my building which said – "Honesty, Quality, and Action". The people believed me and I spent the next fifteen years totally committed to delivering to my people as their Parliamentary leader.

This chapter is dedicated to the hard-working drivers of the Highlands Highway, and all those beautiful people who depend on this mighty road to survive, and to the great people of Lae City and Morobe.

The first cricket team to compete against whites in Port Moresby, 1929 – Makura, Phillip, Doilegu, Merari, Tiraka, Mahuru, Maru, Pita, Aieki – (standing), Alaidi, Charles Abel, Cecil Abel, Gogoadina (seated).

Doctor William J Porteous and staff, Punjab Mission, Shahabad, which relocated to Jagadhri, Northern Punjab, India, 1915.

Chapter 14

The Queen

As I drove into the Lae International Hotel in July of 2005, and parked outside our unit in the Paradise Apartments, I had a sense of dread in my heart. It was another late night at work and the arguments between Hacy and I had gotten worse and worse. As I opened the door slowly there was darkness inside. My wife and three children had left.

"NEVER, EVER tell me what to do!" "F.. off and leave me alone!" I yelled as I slapped my wife across the face and she fell to the bed crying.

It was 3 a.m. in the morning. I had been drinking after work, again. As I slumped on the edge of the bed, I felt my mobile phone smash into my eye and my anger and guilt erupted.

My dear wife, Hacy, and I are probably two excellent candidates for a broken marriage. I grew up with a very difficult mother, and a sense of deep frustration as to why my father did not stand up to her more. In my heart, I vowed many times that no woman would ever tell me what to do.

I had been in love with my girlfriend in Australia and it took me years to get over it.

Hacy felt abandoned by her birth mother when her parents separated. She was abused as a child, and had a difficult time under the regime of her stepmother. Eventually, she ran away from home. I've observed since the day we met, her longing for acceptance and approval from her family.

So, here was I carrying all my baggage and lack of emotional commitment, and Hacy was emotionally insecure and demanding. On top of it, my self-centered, obsessive and compulsive tendencies with work, or music, or sport meant a disaster in the waiting.

As of Easter Sunday this year, 2023, Hacy and I will have been together for 30 years. She is my best friend and the rock of our family. I am so proud of her and the way she has blossomed into a sports administrator, business woman, and community leader. Her patience and commitment to our marriage, and Faith, have won through. She has helped me to become a better man, a better father, and become closer to the person I truly am.

If there is one thing I want to impart to you from this book, and my lessons over four generations, is the importance of the centrality of family to everything.

This is the example passed down through our family history.

On Saturday, the 16th of March 1907, my Great Grandmother, Beatrice Abel wrote from Kwato Island to her husband, Reverend Charles William Abel, who was visiting the outstations in Milne Bay;

"My Own Dear Love,

Your sweet letter arrived just after prayers last night. It was a very sweet surprise my darling. But it seems so long since you went and your letter was written on Monday" **(Abel Papers, New Guinea Collection, Michael Somare Library, UPNG).**

This was a typical tone of the many letters between them.

Twenty-three years later, on Thursday 10th April 1930, after saying quietly "Beatrice", three times, Abel died (from injuries suffered from being hit by a speeding car while walking in Surrey, England). Beatrice was on the other side of the world, at Kwato, at the time.

I've written of the love with which my paternal Grandmother, Sheila Abel, spoke of my late Grandfather, Russell Abel. She wore her wedding band to the end, and spoke of how she looked forward to seeing him again.

Cecil Abel married Semi Bwagagaia in 1951, at a time when mixed racial marriages were very rare and frowned upon. They never separated.

My father stuck with my mother through a difficult and turbulent marriage. He was constantly going out of his way to hold the family together.

We are all attracted to the notion of romantic love. Nearly every song on the radio is about a girl or a boy in love. We write sweet text messages and profess our love in letters. We dream about our girlfriends and boyfriends. But as soon as we are married, all this abruptly ends. It's as if as soon as someone becomes your wife a switch is flicked and she becomes a baby-making machine and punching bag. Your romantic feelings are now only available to someone who is not your wife. It is practically unheard of in PNG for a husband to publicly demonstrate affection for his wife in word, and certainly not in action.

You wooed her heavily before you married her, what happened after she believed your nice words and married you? The romance should be for life! You have married her to make her happy, not miserable. **Make your wife your queen, not your slave.**

Of course, everything applies both ways but I suspect more responsibility (and guilt) lies with the guys!

Your relationship with your spouse and the dedication to this fundamental unit has dramatic repercussions in your life and potentially for generations to come.

There is no more important relationship than that between husband and wife.

"Husbands love your wives, even as Christ also loved the church and gave himself up for it;" **Ephesians 5:25**

Your happiness, the future of your children, and the stability and success of the community and country relies on successful marriages and families. This is not a new concept, but we are not sufficiently committed to it as yet.

Our Faith tells us of that importance, and that it is in giving that we shall receive.

"Give and it shall be given unto you; good measure,.." **Luke 6:38**

This absolutely applies to marriage.

Through the prayers of my wife, I have seen this, and the presence and intention of the Lord more clearly, and it has helped to provide me with the strength and discipline to commit myself to His direction. In doing so, I have seen the blessings in my marriage and in my children. My love for my wife has grown every day. **My love for her has made her more secure and confident, and she has grown into the successful, loving person that she was meant to be.** Our children are well-rounded, confident individuals. This does not mean we did not have our share of tribulations on the way, or still to come!

Our daughters especially, have witnessed the effort and struggle that their parents have put into their marriage. They see the love and respect in the home. They see a strong, tough, but loving mother. This strengthens and resolves them into the future. They realize that women can be leaders as well as mothers. Nikita Badi Abel, the eldest, is a wonderful, dedicated mother to our first grandchild, Aaliyah Courtney Solomon, and has a successful business.

Inner peace and happiness come from the quality of our relationships, not in the endless pursuit of the satisfaction and vanity of the flesh.

One of the greatest temptations for men is that of lust. Sex is a biological urge and one of God's many gifts. As men we need to admit to this powerful desire. **Starting with the truth is one of the bedrock principles of this book.** It is how we deal with all our weaknesses, through love and discipline that is important. It may seem tough to overcome but you will realize that the resulting blessings and happiness from a commitment to your spouse are much greater. The same principles apply to building anything of real value. We tend to realize this too late in life, after all the mistakes.

I recommend that you don't rush into marriage. Enjoy your single status in a responsible manner while you can. When you finally get married be prepared to make a lifelong commitment and mean it. The sex gets better and better in a loving relationship by the way!

One of the things that I've learned is **not to impose my standards and views on my wife**. It's not about me, it's about what makes her happy. I used to nag Hacy about exercise and losing weight because I place such a high priority on physical fitness and discipline.

I am not an easy person to live with because I am still driven by 'my demons.' That's my problem, not hers.

I understand now that many of my words only upset her and make her feel unhappy. I love my wife regardless of these things, and the imposition of my views on her is not reflecting this. I want her to be happy, feel beautiful, and loved. So, I always hold her hand, put my arm around her in church, and kiss and hug her constantly in front of my children. **A few loving words and touch every day are so powerful**, as are selfish and hurtful words.

Of course, marriage is a partnership. **It works both ways.** There will be frustration, if it seems that you are doing all the right things, but your spouse is not responding. It takes prayer, patience, and work like all things of value. I must say that there is a point where responsible love must be exercised. **Blind love and dedication can be very harmful.**

One of Hacy's strengths is the courage to confront and deal with issues head on. Many of us will shy away from confrontation and allow issues to fester, and long-term damage is then done.

I wish my father had dealt with the presence of alcohol in our home. It seemed that it was just too difficult to deal with. We would have family meetings to talk about what was a very obvious problem, and the solution was so apparent – no more drinking in our home. But that decision was never made by the head of the house. As such, we carried on as if there was no problem. This caused tremendous psychological trauma on us as children. This was despite the fact that our father was a wonderfully dedicated and loving man.

Loving your spouse does not mean they can do anything they like.

My drinking, in combination with my insecurities and childhood experiences, was prompting behaviour that was bad for the family. The answer was simple – I had to stop drinking, and I did.

Many of us use alcohol as an excuse for bad behavior. We can't seem to function in a social setting without drinking. To give up is much too difficult. When I say to people at a party, "No thanks, I can enjoy myself without drinking", they look at me as if something is wrong with me! Yet most of our social problems with domestic violence, financial problems, marriage breakups, car accidents, child abuse, can be related back to alcohol.

Hacy would react with harsh and emotional outbursts, that would often take me by surprise, and hurt my feelings. I would respond emotionally as well, and find ways to defend myself and blame her. When I took an honest look at myself first and made the effort to change, she also made an effort, and changed.

If we are serious about our children and our marriages, we must be honest with ourselves and take the necessary steps out of love to exercise discipline and eliminate the source of the problem. **We must act out of tough, responsible love.**

I was downstairs at home one beautiful Saturday in our home at Top Town suburb in Alotau. I heard a voice from the back fence calling out, "Uncle, uncle, come and see Coco!"

For some reason I always automatically assume the worst when I hear such tone of voice. It was 2003, and Courtney Henao Abel, our second born, was six years old. She was playing with Jemima Orake at the house behind us. I suppressed my thoughts and ran to the fence.

Coco was looking at me through the chainmesh. She raised her foot and said, "Look at my toe Daddy"

I glanced down and nearly fainted. Half of her big toe on her left foot was gone and I could see the bone sticking out. She was not crying. A nerve must have been severed, I guess.

She looked at me with innocent eyes as her Dad, and hero, who could solve anything. Missing toe, no worries just show Dad and he'll fix it!

I sprinted around and through the embers of the burning kunai grass on the vacant block next door and lifted Coco.

"Don't look at it baby, everything is going to be ok," I said with tears in my eyes.

My overactive brain was already 100 miles ahead – Sew toe back on? Infection? Which doctor? Will she be able to walk properly again???!

Under the neighbour's house was a large hessian bag full of second-hand clothes. To keep the top of this bag securely closed they had placed there a four-litre paint tin, filled with concrete. The kids had pulled on the bag and the tin rolled over and crashed down onto Coco's foot, cutting off half her big toe against the concrete floor.

As I rushed her to the hospital and into the emergency ward, I was so relieved to see Doctor Barry Kirby (the now flying doctor) there. "Let me have a look," he said, and removed the cloth I had placed over the wound. I felt nauseous and sweaty.

"Please Doctor help my baby.."

He took a look at my face and asked, "Are you ok?"

"I will be when you fix my baby!", I said.

They tried to patch Coco's toe back together from what remained of it but it went black after several days. They had to remove the dead tissue and took some skin from her leg and covered the toe. She was so strong and brave throughout – as she is to this day, being admitted to the Legal Bar recently as Counsellor Courtney Abel.

She still only has half a big toe..

All children are the most precious things in the world. Once you bring a child into the world, the game changes. As a minimum, they deserve a committed Mum and Dad in their corner. The biggest gift you can give your child is the foundational, unconditional, but responsible love in their formative years. This is best represented by being present in their lives in the first instance. The example you demonstrate each day imprints these impressionable young minds – how do Dad and Mum speak to each other? How do they speak of others?

Establish the principles of love, honesty, discipline, and responsibility through your actions from the outset. Your wise words must be backed up with your wise deeds!

Do not neglect your children but also do not dote on them. One of the hardest things for a parent is letting your child go, giving them the tools to fly independently from the nest. Our need to be loved and attached to our children can override the responsibility to take some tough decisions to expose them to the real world for their own good.

Our family's recent experience with the disbursement of my father's estate has exposed some of the potential downsides of leaving some wealth behind for your children, or making them too reliant on you when you are still around.

There is irresponsible love or selfish love, and responsible love. Sometimes, we may seem to be acting out of the best interests of others through our constant generosity. Our intentions may be genuine, or may be misguided in that we are subconsciously feeding off the dependency of others for our own self-validation. This then can have a debilitating effect on the recipient.

It is probably best not to bequeath significant financial assets to your children. If you are lucky enough to be in a position to do so, and choose to, make sure you have a Will and that it is absolutely clear as to the distribution of your estate. Arguments over inherited money can destroy family unity.

The constant love, quality formal education, and family legacy were the most precious gifts we received from our father, and our forebears. We have a responsibility to do the same for our children.

Hacy Henao Abel, 1995.

Nikita Abel, Courtney Abel, Hacy Abel, Jordan Abel, Charles K. Abel,
2003.

Charles K. Abel, Hacy Abel, Courtney Abel, Jordan Abel, and Nikita Abel – 2021.

Chapter 15

I Need My Son

It was around 8 p.m. that evening as I drove my Nissan Navara up the hill after closing up the business for the day. My tired mind wandered aimlessly on another day of operating a small business running taxi cabs, a pool room, and a cafeteria, in a building that I had just finished building in the heart of town. Jordan, my son was sitting patiently in the back seat, he was four years old. He had always been such a calm and patient child (and adult), unlike his father.

We turned off the main road and into our street at Top Town suburb and turned left again to arrive at the picket gate in front of the house, pausing to allow the guard to open the gate. It was a night like any other. There was a sudden explosion of glass on my right as the window shattered all over me.

"Get out now!!" the blur outside my door yelled. My mind was racing trying to catch up to events. There was a shotgun touching the side of my head. I tried to calm myself and think!

Jordan is in the back seat, I could hear my inner voice whisper, then shout, then scream! I gathered myself and as confidently as I could, opened the door and stepped out. There were three men with their noses and mouths covered by shirts tied around their heads. The other two had machetes.

"Please take the car, but *I need my son* in the back seat." I said firmly.

"Shut up and move!" the gunman replied and jumped into the driver's seat. My heart jolted. Did he hear what I said??

I moved without thinking or seeing anything except my son. I reached through the broken window and behind the new driver's head to unlock the back seat door, opened the door as the others were jumping into the car from the other side, and grabbed my precious boy. I realized he was crying loudly. I just threw him to my chest and jumped away. Thank you Lord.

The car jerked forward, stopped and jerked again into reverse, before screeching away down the street.

My crashed and abandoned vehicle was recovered by the police at Goilanai that very night. It was May 2007, an election year in Papua New Guinea.

I went to visit Dad in his office two days later. You had to wade through the busy front office and people waiting to see him, then through the piles of paper and books as you entered.

"Dad, its election year, have you ever thought about standing for Parliament?" I asked him finally. "You have helped just about everyone in Milne Bay in one way or another. You have a good chance don't you think?"

He said, "Look Charlie, I know you are shaken by the nasty incident recently, and thank God you and Jordan are safe, but I don't like politics and I never have. I can't see myself ever standing for Parliament. It's a dirty game."

I left him to his papers and line of visitors and made my way home, not really sure why I had broached the subject with Dad. I had never had the remotest thought about politics in the past.

The next morning, I sat bolt upright in bed, turned to my best friend, and said, "I'm standing in the election."

Hacy said, "Sale', we have just taken out a big loan to build Chascorp Haus and start a business. We have no savings left. What are you doing?"

2011 was a tumultuous year in Papua New Guinean politics to say the least. Grand Chief and founding father of the country, and the incumbent Prime Minister, Sir Michael Somare, lay in his sick bed in Raffles Hospital in Singapore. He had been absent for more than six months and the Acting Prime Minister was Sam Abal, who had previously been the Minister for Foreign Affairs in the National Alliance Party-led Government.

The National Alliance (NA) Party had been effectively in power since 2002, and was the first Government to survive a full term of five years, and had almost completed a second full term. It was a result of the effect of the new Organic Law on Political Parties and Candidates (OLIPAC) that Prime Minister, Sir Mekere Morauta, had introduced in his short tenure from 1999 to 2002. This law restricted the ability of MPs to abandon their political parties, in the free-for-all that ensued when the 18-month grace period for a new Prime Minister lapsed.

The provision in the *Constitution* for an opportunity for a Motion of No Confidence in an incumbent Prime Minister, after 18 months in office, effectively meant that no government had survived a full tenure since Independence in 1975. Sir Mekere intended to strengthen the political party system to promote stability and the development of proper institutionalized political parties with clear ideological platforms. The subsequent mandate from an election was then protected somewhat from the vicissitudes of PNG's version of democracy.

OLIPAC was subsequently deemed unconstitutional by the Supreme Court, and we were essentially back to the 'good old days'.

The prelude to the events of 2011 started in mid-2010. I was the Tourism, Culture, and Arts Minister, and a member of the NA Party, whom I joined after winning my first election in 2007 as an Independent. Sir John Luke Crittin was elected Governor of Milne Bay Province, and Gordon Wesley was returned as Member for Samarai-Murua. We were all Independent MPs from Milne Bay. By virtue of the three of us joining NA in the Kokopo Camp in 2007, I negotiated the Tourism Ministry. The MP for Angoram and political numbers man for NA, Arthur Somare, had promised the Fisheries Ministry as well for Gordon but he turned it down in return for some projects for Samarai-Murua. I had worked hard for these two ministries and was naturally disappointed.

Sir Puka Temu was the Deputy Prime Minister and Minister for Lands and Mining. He was one of the four deputy parliamentary leaders for NA, representing the Southern Region, of which Milne Bay Province is a part.

According to the NA Party's *Constitution*, the party leader can only serve a maximum of two parliamentary terms. Sir Michael Somare was approaching the end of his second term as leader of NA, and the issue was raised in the party caucus as to the process whereby a new leader is elected. It would seem appropriate that this issue should be dealt with in good time before the 2012 National Elections.

In anticipation of a vacancy in the party leadership, the MP for Vanimo Green and Forestry Minister at the time, Belden Namah, and I, decided to support Sir Puka Temu for the party leadership. Following successive meetings of the Party, it became apparent from the 'heavies' in the parliamentary wing and party executive that any leadership change would not be entertained.

With the Supreme Court ruling the OLIPAC unconstitutional on the 7th of July 2010, what began as internal rumblings within the NA party blew into a revolt when Sir Puka, Namah, and I walked out of the party and teamed up with the Opposition to mount a motion of no confidence against Somare.

My genuine intention had always been to support an organized internal change in the NA Party, not to pursue a motion against the Prime Minister. It came as a surprise to me when the Opposition joined us.

It goes without saying that our family had historical ties to the Somare family. I served as a Minister under Sir Michael for four years, and it was an honour. I had applied myself fully as the Minister for Culture and Tourism, implementing the Tourism Masterplan (2007–2017), developing and launching the PNG Cruise Ship Strategy, protecting and walking the Kokoda Track, and advocating for direct flights into tourism zones.

Our misconstrued attempt at a motion of no confidence in 2010 failed and I tendered my resignation as Minister and retreated to the back bench.

When Somare was facing a leadership tribunal in December of 2010 and stood down, he appointed Sam Abal, the Member for Wabag, as Deputy Prime Minister and Acting Prime Minister in his absence. Sam invited me back into Cabinet as Minister Assisting the Prime Minister. We were still members of the National Alliance Party.

From late 2010 to late 2011, after a year with an Acting Prime Minister, the situation became untenable, leading to the parliamentary revolt, and on the 2nd of August 2011, Peter O'Neill became Prime Minister, after Parliament declared a vacancy in the seat of the Prime Minister.

At this stage, Somare had been receiving medical treatment since April 2011, with heart issues, which required valve surgery in Singapore. His seat in Parliament had been declared vacant because of his three consecutive absences from Parliamentary sittings.

I had moved with my fellow Southern Region MPs of the National Alliance Party into the 'camp' at Sir Mekere's residence on Touaguba Hill. We were asked to nominate a new leader for National Alliance amongst ourselves and Don Polye, the Member for Kandep was elected. I then left the National Alliance Party and joined the Peoples National Congress Party (PNC).

I became the Minister for Trade and Commerce in the government that took the country to the 2012 National Elections. Belden Namah, the Member for Vanimo Green was the Deputy Prime Minister and Minister for Forests. The constitutional crisis and political machinations of this period are ample fodder for a whole other book.

PNC came out of the 2012 National Elections with 27 MPs and was invited to form the next government. Peter O'Neill was Prime Minister and Leo Dion from the Triumph Heritage Empowerment Party became Deputy Prime Minister. I became the Minister for National Planning, and held this post until the 2017 National Elections.

In August 2017, I had just been declared for a third time as the Member for Alotau Open. For the third time in the past ten years, we had begun to congregate in Alotau Town from around the country, which included the various coalition factions and Independent MPs as they concluded their respective counts.

I was the incumbent Planning Minister in the PNC Party led coalition government, under Prime Minister Peter O'Neill. As in 2012, I was hosting the formation of the government in my Alotau District, and home province of Milne Bay on behalf of the PNC Party, of which I was a senior member by then.

It was in fairly advanced stages of the political process now with the necessary numbers intact to form government. The formulation of the Alotau Accord 2 was in advanced stages, and discussions had turned to the composition of the new Cabinet.

As we strolled along one of the footpaths on the grounds of the Airways Hotel (now Bayside Hotel), the Prime Minister pulled me closer and said, "Charles, I'm deciding about who will be Deputy Prime Minister. We will keep it in the Party this time. There are several options but we have to consider regional balance as well as seniority and capability. I think that you should be the Treasurer, but you would also make a good Deputy Prime Minister. Are you interested? It is one or the other."

I said, "My preference is Treasury, Prime Minister, but you have a difficult task of looking after everyone so I'll allow you to decide in the best interests of our government."

I had been offered the Planning Ministry in the 2011 Government, then it was changed to the Petroleum Ministry, and then I ended up with Commerce and Trade, so I was familiar with the process of trying to please a large coalition and Government Caucus.

I was surprised at the breakfast meeting the next morning when the PM announced that I would be the next Treasurer and Deputy Prime Minister in the O'Neill/Abel Government.

So began my tenure as Deputy PM and Treasurer. I believe I was the first MP to serve both roles concurrently.

On the 11th of April 2019, one year and nine months later, James Marape, the Finance Minister, and Member for Tari Pori resigned as minister, which precipitated a collapse of the PNC Party, led to a vote of no confidence, and the election of Marape as Prime Minister on the 30th May 2019, under the PANGU Party banner.

Such is PNG politics..

Charles K. Abel, The Lowy Institute, Sydney, 2018

Charles K. Abel welcoming Chinese President Xi Jinping to APEC in 2018.

Chapter 16

On Hands and Knees

We had come to a halt at the top of the Owen Stanley Range, at a point exactly between the north and south coasts of the District of Alotau. It was the 21st of December 2021. I opened the door and got out of the mud stained, 10-seater Toyota Landcruiser that I was driving. My District Administrator was walking back up the steep track ahead of me and he looked very worried.

"Boss, the Police Commander just shouted at me. He said it is too far and we should turn back."

"Let me talk to him," I said.

I took the slippery walk down to where the Police Commander and his vehicle and troops were halted.

"Leader," he said. "Sorry, but this is too far and dangerous. We have been misled about the road conditions. My men and I need to get back to Alotau."

"Commander," I replied. "I'm really sorry about the condition of this new road. I think the recent rain storms have unfortunately made it much worse than we thought. You can all head back. I will never turn around. If I have to, I will crawl down to Mainawa *on my hands and knees*."

The Commander looked me in the eyes and slowly a smile came across his worried face.

"Leader if you say we go, then we go. We are with you all the way."

As we lit fires by the roadside that night to ward off the mountain cold and mist, I couldn't help but wonder again about the consequences of just one car going over the edge. The road was incredibly dangerous with several places with ravines on both sides. We had only got this far with the support of two D6 Caterpiller bulldozers. Even they had got bogged several times. On top of this, we had been threatened by criminal gangs, and by claims, that there are 'supernatural forces that will stop you breaking a road to the Rabaraba coast'.

My wife and only son, Jordan, were with me and several of my Council Presidents. Many of them had fear and doubt in their eyes.

At one point earlier that day, after the bulldozers had worked for two hours to clear a landslip, it was my turn to rev the engine and take a run at the flimsy log bridge over the creek and up the muddy embankment. I had the oldest vehicle and the tyres were half bald. I cursed myself for not having my usual foresight to double check everything. I barely made it twenty metres up the slope before sliding back to the edge of the creek in a cloud of engine fumes.

The bulldozer trundled down in reverse, and we attached the tow rope. I instructed Hacy, Jordan, and the other passengers to disembark to lighten the load.

We began to struggle to the top with my tyres spinning and the old chassis being dragged reluctantly forward. It became steeper and steeper and the tow rope began to make complaining noises. The tension was rising and the sweat dripping. When the rope snapped, I thought I was done for. I nearly pushed the brakes through the floor and ripped out the handbrake. The vehicle went backwards against the spinning tyres and brakes. The danger was the risk of sliding sideways and rolling all the way to the bottom.

I opened my lungs and yelled as I worked the brakes. The truck slowed and stopped. "Maybe this road was not meant to be?" I thought, yet again.

For ten years we had been working to open this 130-kilometre road through the mountains to connect the provincial capital, Alotau, to the District Headquarters of Rabaraba Station, on the north coast of the mainland for the first time.

I had initially walked the road in 2009, starting at Givari on the north coast and walking inland to Kwabunaki, to see if it was possible to bring the existing road along the coast from the east, and around Girumea Point to Wedau. This point is the main obstacle to the road from Alotau continuing along the coast from the east, to reach Wedau, and then Rabaraba.

Girumea Point rises 300 metres from the ocean in a series of sheer cliffs that extend for three or four kilometres, making the construction of a road impossible. The alternative was to tunnel through the rock, or extend the existing road from Topura, and go inland and around Girumea, before descending back to the coast to Givari Village, through the village of Kwabunaki.

It was obvious from the steep descent from behind Girumea to Kwabunaki, and several sharp ridges and deep ravines between Kwabunaki and the coast, that this route was out of the question.

From Kwabunaki, we walked to Wedau and spent the night. The next day we walked inland to Mainawa to investigate the possible route directly over the mountains to Alotau in a north to south direction.

At Mainawa we overnighted. The people killed a pig for us and the next morning I packed pig grease and squeezed lemon juice into a jar that I had brought. I plastered my legs before we left, and kept plastering after crossing every river, of which there were many. This was to deter the many leeches that stretched out from the bushes as we brushed past. We would spend time at each rest stop removing them with salt and knives.

We walked eleven hours through thick jungle following an old overgrown track that often disappeared, before sleeping in the rain by the Sagabada River. Another six hours later we arrived at an old logging road at Naura, where we were able to be picked up by vehicle and return to Alotau. This seemed to be the only viable option for a possible road to service the people of the north coast, northern islands, and ultimately link Milne Bay Province to Oro Province.

The next thing was to establish a pilot track, and the Alotau District hired two bulldozers and set about doing this.

It took until April of 2017 for the pilot track to reach Mainawa, from Narau on the Alotau side of the mountain range. So, on the 12th of April, we set off with our convoy, full of hope of driving through to Dogura/Wedau on the north coast for the first time.

We made it as far as the Gumini River where we camped for the night. The following day brough heavy rain and in the struggle to cross the river, all of the seven-vehicle convoy, except one, had to turn back. We proceeded with an old Toyota Hilux and a D6 bulldozer, until only the bulldozer could continue. I placed my family (Hacy and Jordan again) on the bulldozer with all the solar lamps that we were delivering, and I ran alongside them in the mud and rain for several hours.

When we reached Gavi my blood pressure erupted because it was literally 100 metres of sheer cliff sides on a razor stone ridge. The left-hand side actually caved inward as you looked over the edge. I told everyone to get off the bulldozer and held my breath as it made its way over with the ground shaking beneath us. I have no idea how this part of the road was cut by the operator. I could barely walk over it with my eyes open.

It wasn't long before we came upon the second bulldozer. It was buried in mud trying to get down the last slope to Mainawa. We had to walk from there down to Mainawa, and overnight. I was picked up from Mainawa by chopper to meet the Deputy Prime Minister, Leo Dion at Dogura. We had constructed a memorial to the late Sir John Guise and the late Sir Kingsford Dibela, next to the famous Anglican cathedral, overlooking Wamira Bay and Girumea Point, and I had invited the Deputy PM to open it.

On the 22nd of December 2021, on the second attempt, we finally drove through with ten vehicles (and two bulldozers) to Mainawa, and on to Dogura and Wedau, after forty-eight hours without sleep. It was history in the making and demonstrated that it was physically possible to build a road through those mountains (and so-called spiritual impediments).

I explained to the people of Wedau, not only the obvious significance of having the road broken through to the north coast, but the importance of committed leadership.

I had been to Dogura and Wedau probably fifty times previously. We had built the concrete jetty there, the permanent water supply, funded the high school and the primary school, provided a 50 kva generator, subsidized the construction of the communication tower, provided two tractors, presented the Anglican Church with a forty-foot work boat – the *Alotau 1*, dinghies, chainsaws, solar lighting, and roofing iron to every council ward.

One of my main objectives, as a leader, was to break the mould and give some hope to our people, by actually sticking to my commitments and working every day to make a difference in their lives.

The Alotau District is one of the biggest in the country, with seven local-level governments, and 157 council wards. It has nineteen different language groups, and these people live along hundreds of kilometres of coast line and way up into the rugged Owen Stanley Range.

I approached the daunting task of bringing services to them by following a simple 'service delivery framework' that eventually became a part of the *National Planning and Monitoring Act* when I became the Planning Minister.

In concert with the District Service Improvement Program funding of 10 million Kina per year, and the establishment of the District Development Authorities, we delivered hundreds of impact projects against the service delivery framework. The framework basically comprises a hub and spoke configuration of 'services delivery centres' linked by a transport and communication network.

My plan was to systematically upgrade and build the transport and communication system as the first priority, because every other activity relies so heavily on these. We upgraded the Alotau Town roads as the provincial capital, sealed the highway to East Cape, upgraded the north coast highway, maintained the oil palm roads, connected the main highway to Fife Bay on the south coast, upgraded the Sirisiri-Agaun Road, and broke the pilot road through to the Rabaraba Coast, as already described.

We built seven concrete jetties at strategic locations, and provided the mainline churches with fiberglass forty-foot work boats being, *MV Alotau 1* (Anglican), *Alotau 2* (United), *Alotau 4* (Kwato), *Alotau 5* (Catholic), and *MV Alotau 3* to the District Administration itself.

Tractors and trailers were supplied to the council wards to service the various feeder roads. All coastal wards received a fibre-glass dinghy and outboard motor.

We sponsored Dr. Barry Kirby, and his flying doctor operation, to service the airstrips at Rabaraba, Tarakwaruru, and Agaun.

The district then subsidized, to the tune of K250 000 each, nine Digicel towers to be established at key locations, such as all the local-level government headquarters. We established VHF radios at all our health centres.

The service delivery centres within this network comprised the Provincial Headquarters at the hub (at a national level the Provincial Headquarters linked to the Regional Headquarters, then the national capital), connecting to the District HQs to the LLG HQs to the Zone HQs, and to the Ward HQs.

At each of these locations we invested into minimum service levels of Administration, Education, Health, and Law and Justice. For example, every LLG HQ was to have a high school, and we built the James Chalmers Memorial High School at Fife Bay, and the Cape Vogel High School at Tarakwaruru. Every Zone HQ was to have a primary school, and every Ward an elementary school.

We also subsidized the prices of copra, cocoa, and coffee, and supplied oil palm seedlings for free to farmers.

It would bore you to outline the hundreds of projects we delivered. Importantly as well, we always endeavored to ensure that the assets which were purchased went to the churches or a government agency, such as the local-level government or council ward. The only things received by individuals were solar lamps, water tanks, chicken wire and hatchlings, and roofing iron, which were distributed on a household basis. In financial terms, these were minimal, relative to the main projects.

The other important factor was that the Alotau District was always at the top in terms of compliance with all acquittal and reporting requirements. We were subject to a full audit by the Department of Finance, and Office of Rural Development.

I never planned to get into politics. I thought I was a businessman. After making the bold and sudden announcement to Hacy in May 2007, I had to get cracking, as there was only two months to go before voting was to commence. I had no money left after building 'Chascorp Haus' when we returned from Lae in 2006.

There were thirty-nine candidates for the Alotau Open seat in 2007 and we somehow managed to win by 305 votes.

I immediately set out to be the best Member the Alotau people had ever seen. I was totally determined to show that a leader can be committed, honest, and produce real outcomes to improve people's lives.

The people of Alotau Open returned me in two subsequent elections and I sincerely hope I did them proud in Parliament and on the ground. It was my absolute honour to serve them for fifteen years.

Alotau District transport and infrastructure programs, 2007 -2022.

Chapter 17

The Witch

There was a tremendous buzzing in my ears such that I could hear nothing else, and it was freezing cold. Something was terribly wrong. My eyes rolled instantly to the foot of my bed, or should I say mat separating me from the earth floor. There stood an old woman, dressed entirely in black, staring intently at me. There was an unmistakable aura and power flowing from her and I felt a wave of terror sweep over me. I tried to sit up and scream at the same time. I could not move, no matter how hard I tried. It was as if everything was suspended, including time itself. I watched my visitor slowly raise a dark sheet and move to cover me with it. I say with all honesty that the simple words that came to my mind were, "Jesus is with me.." Despite all my family history and traditions, I had never been particularly religious, but these words were instantaneous.

The old woman seemed to hesitate, she raised her sheet several times and found it difficult to complete her task. The words kept repeating in my mind as my wild eyes stared. Eventually, she turned and left the room. I tried and tried but could not move until about ten minutes later when the humming subsided. I staggered out to the fire and without an explanation woke all the guys and told them to sit around me until morning.

There was no doubt in my mind the next morning as I examined the eyes of the first village people in the morning, the unusual inquisitiveness in one of them in particular. I gave no power to them by holding my tongue. I pretended everything was normal. Following breakfast, we walked to the chapel and I asked the Pastor to bless our team. As he prayed, the tears flowed uncontrollably from my eyes. I did not tell him why.

It was on my first campaign trail during the 2017 General Election that I was attacked by a series of supernatural events that crystalized certain scattered views I had held and suspicions about my horrific childhood sleep patterns.

The most powerful occurrence was at Menapi Village, Cape Vogel, in the Rabaraba District. It was a culmination of a strange series of events that commenced with some 'threats' I received before departing Alotau.

With *Orina* anchored offshore and the day's welcome and speeches were done, I was allocated a room of my own in the chief's hut, and my team of twelve or so guys were to sleep around the fire outside. We had our meal with the elders of the village and had some relaxed discussions with *buai* and smokes all around. I was somewhat exhausted following a difficult trip to Baiawa at the Oro Province border, and was still recovering from a bad bout of malaria.

I retired to my room alone and was soon fast asleep. What happened next is forever burned into my memory. I awoke to a somewhat familiar feeling but at a level of power I'd never felt before.

As we left Sirisiri about a week earlier, at midnight so that we could get around Sibiribiri Point (Cape Vogel), and make it to Baiawa, on the Oro Province border that coming day, the boys came to me and said, "Boss, we are being followed by some floating red eyes".

I said, "What? Stop believing in nonsense."

It was a beautiful moonlit night and the sea was like glass. I was relieved that we had calm seas to get around the infamous Sibiribiri, which was usually very rough at this time of year. Little did I suspect of what was to happen. As we approached Wabubu Village and Sibiribiri after two hours there was an almost unbelievable and dramatic change in the weather. The wind suddenly began to pick up and *Orina* began to pitch. I awoke and went to the wheelhouse. The clouds had rolled over the moon. The skipper said, "Boss, look at the lights." I turned to the beach on the left-hand side, to see three or four flashing lights. Out of the corner of my eye I saw something on my right, so I turned to see several lights flashing on the seaward side as well. I felt my heart beat faster. It was raining heavily by now and the boat was pitching more and more against a strong headwind and swell. We then lost all visibility. I quickly looked to the compass; it was spinning out of control. For a minute everything seemed to go into slow motion. Panic squeezed my chest.

"Give me the spotlight!" I yelled, and raced to the front of the boat.

I could barely keep my feet. I shone ahead but could not see five metres beyond a wall of rain, then instantly I shone downward to the sea below – **we were on the reef.** "Swing!!" I screamed, shooting my arm to the right.

As the skipper swung, we were hit by a huge breaking wave three-quarters on the bow. The boat lifted, almost rolled and righted itself. I scrambled back to the wheelhouse.

"Head directly into the waves and keep going!"

As the lighting struck, I turned and saw the outline of the land close behind us.

The passengers were all screaming and crying. I told everyone to put on life jackets and hang on. We slowly made our way out into the open sea, climbing up and down each wave, between Cape Vogel and Ferguson Island. I told the skipper to hold the boat into the wind until daylight. I looked at the clock, it was 5 a.m.

"We are in Your Hands." I lay down and closed my eyes.

As day broke, the wind only seemed to pick up again. We ploughed forward in an attempt to round Cape Vogel. I could see the line of old ship wrecks on the famous point. Our 23-foot dinghy was somehow still attached to the boat but as the wind turned behind us the waves started to throw the dinghy forward. Suddenly, it rushed towards the stern, came over the stern platform, and crashed into the back of the cabin sending our passengers scattering. As the dinghy jerked back to sea again the tether rope snapped and it floated free. I grabbed the red fuel tank and threw it into the sea, gave the fuel line and key to a crew man and told him to swim for the dinghy as the *Orina* idled.

The escaped dinghy was recaptured and he followed us to calmer waters beyond the point.

We were able to get to Baiawa and visited Yarame, Midino, Tapio and Pem Villages over the next few days as we made our way back towards the Cape again. We wanted to visit Magabara before getting to Mukawa and Bogaboga. We approached the beach at Magabara and walked into the village some ten minutes in from the shoreline. The village was absolutely deserted and we wandered around until we saw a young girl seated beside her mother who was lying under a blanket on a platform beside their hut. The girl told me that everybody was in the garden. I asked what was wrong with her mother and she said, "Village sickness."

I said, "Take her to the health centre".

She muttered, "Already, it's no good."

I looked down at the mother. Her eyes were glassy. I wanted to give some sort of assurance so I gently held her by the hand and said, "God is more powerful than anything, and He will heal you, don't worry." We quietly left the village.

That night I became very feverish. We were totally out of medicines and my great friend, the late Pilikesa Manimua, gave me the last two Panadols from his basket. I physically could not get up over the next two days. As the boat anchored off Bogaboga, I told the band to go ashore and play for the people. Everyone left for the shore and I was alone on the boat, sweating and shivering under my blanket. As the wind changed against the direction of the current, the *Orina* began to roll badly. I could not get up and my kidneys felt like they were bursting. I suffered terribly until the team returned after midnight and reset the anchor.

We visited Menapi as I was slowly recovering and had the **'the witch'** experience there.

Finally, after twenty-one days at sea we returned to Alotau. The only thing on my mind was a drink with ice in it! I returned to Cape Vogel sometime later, as the newly elected MP for Alotau, having totally forgotten about the Magabara incident. A lady quietly approached me and asked if I remembered her and I shook my head. She was the lady that lay on her sickbed the last time we were there and she had recovered.

In the late 1970s we moved to our house on the edge of KB Mission. This house is located directly in the 'war corridor' which runs from Ahioma in the east to *No.3 Strip* at Rabe, following the road that still exists today. This was a battleground for two weeks in the Battle of Milne Bay. Hundreds of Japanese soldiers were killed, and many allied forces and locals were also killed by the Japanese. Some of them were murdered in horrific ways as reported from investigations after the war.

Sir William Webb, Chief Justice of the Supreme Court of Queensland, provided a **Report on Japanese Atrocities and Breaches of the Rules of Warfare** to Dr. Herbert Evatt, the Minister for External Affairs (Foreign Minister), in 1944. Despite the relatively short period in Milne Bay, the Japanese without justification (not killed in the ordinary course of war), killed thirty-eight Australian soldiers. In the main they were tied up with signal wire and used for bayonet practice. At least fifty-nine native men and women were murdered in a calculated manner. Sir William Webb said that in every case the killing was carried out with savage brutality. The women staked out on the ground were raped then mutilated.

My brothers and I were in early primary school starting at Alotau Primary School, then Australian correspondence school with our grandmother, Sheila Abel. By the time Dad had helped establish the Alotau International School, we were living at the KB Mission house where my parents reside to this day (Dad has since passed away).

I was in Grades Four, Five, and Six when living at this location, before going to boarding school in Toowoomba, Queensland, for Grade Seven.

My brothers and I would play in the grounds around the house and find all kinds of war mementos such as bullets, rusted helmets, and interestingly, a lot of Japanese trinkets including female combs and basic jewelry. It was not that unusual in those days as old barges, jeeps, bunkers and the like were strewn all around the bay. We did not think that much of it at the time.

From the moment we took up residence in the ground floor bedroom, with Dad and Mum upstairs, I was plagued by the most horrific nightmares. Many times, my parents would have to come down into the garden at night to take me back into the house. I was sleepwalking and saying strange things. They would be afraid to wake me.

I remember many nights sleeping outside my parents' door. I was terrified of going to sleep. When Mum left the door unlocked sometimes, I would sneak in and sleep under their bed. I wanted to be close to my father, where I felt safe.

The nightmares went away when I left for Toowoomba, but then the homesickness took over!

There were two vivid moments in Australia where I was 'visited'. One was in a hotel on the Darling Downs and the other was at my brother, Jeff's house, in Darwin. I did not get any sleep at the hotel in the first incident. In the second one, I saw an old aboriginal man watching me in the mirror and through the window at night. When I asked my brother the next day, he explained that it was an old aboriginal gravesite. I moved to stay at a hotel instead.

I accompanied my Bubu (granduncle) Haro to the bottom of the garden at the KB residence one day and witnessed him chanting a slow and steady beat. It wasn't long before a bird appeared and seemed to be signing back to him. I was able to clearly sense the humming presence of a force, waxing and waning, as it moved.

I can only relate what I have experienced with no particular explanation except that there is a spiritual dimension that can be interacted with at certain moments. These spirits move with an intent which is mostly born out of curiosity rather than malice. They have a particular aura which is unmistakable and disturbs your consciousness in a profound way. Even when the intent is not malicious, it is extremely unsettling and unpleasant. The presence seems to open a portal of fear and horror.

I can see how the manipulation of this source in combination with people's fear can cause psychological impacts leading to physical manifestations like self-harm or death.

I have felt over the years that I've taken increasing control over the situation by affirming more consciously my faith and belief in a higher power that is good. This affirmation process is a part of a spiritual journey we are all undertaking, whether we are aware of it or not. This journey is a progression towards that which is right and good, and proximity to God. There is a clear sense of this in the spiritual realm.

Alternatively, we can digress in the opposite direction towards obsession with self and subsequent pursuit of all things that satisfy the appetite of the physical senses and ego. Most of human suffering is caused by this digression. The past has many good examples of 'leaders' lost in total obsession with themselves and the preservation of their power. The present Ukraine War is an example of the sacrifice of thousands of innocent people for the satisfaction of one man.

This faith also engenders the discipline to begin to master the physical dimension and all its distractions. Part of our blessing is that with a conscious mind we have a physical being through which we freely exercise that consciousness. We progress our spiritual journey by overcoming our physical weaknesses, particularly, that of selfishness and malevolence, and performing works of good that help alleviate unnecessary suffering. We do this not for reward but out of a sense of love and union with the higher power.

True peace and satisfaction are found the closer to this path you travel. Having said that, I am making some progress but still have a very long way to go!

Charles K. Abel, electoral visit, 2020.

Hacy Abel and Charles Abel on the Mainawa-Kapurika Road,
June 2017.

Jordan Abel and Hacy Abel, camping on the Mainawa-Kapurika Road,
June 2017.

Chapter 18

Reaching for the Stars

"Humanity has a choice — cooperate or perish," Mr. Guterres told delegates, urging them to accelerate the transition from fossil fuels and speed funding to poorer countries struggling under climate impacts that have already occurred. **(COP27 UN Secretary General, Antonio Guterres, 7th November 2022).**

Despite decades of climate talks so far, countries have failed to reduce global greenhouse gas emissions, and their pledges to do so in the future are insufficient to keep the climate from warming to a level that many scientists have said would be catastrophic.

My country Papua New Guinea suffers deeply from the simple inability to benefit from historical precedent and responding to the truth rather than political propaganda. This affliction is not limited to my country. It is the basis of the National Strategy for Responsible Sustainable Development (**StaRS**) that I initiated as National Planning Minister, and the Department of National Planning published in 2016.

It continues to amaze me how even educated constituencies in First World countries such as the United States of America (USA) remain so gullible to political propaganda, based on nationalism and other imperatives that are unfounded or simply untrue.

"US election in a couple of days. THE WORLD NEEDS BETTER LEADERSHIP MORE THAN EVER. International politics has seen a trend towards nationalism, driven by fear and hate, narcissistic leadership. Even the USA has seen democracy undermined by a President suppressing voter rights, stacking the Supreme Court and refusing to commit to an orderly transition of power."

On the 31st of October 2020, several days before the US Presidential elections, I posted on Facebook and Instagram this message about Donald Trump. It was during the 2020 US elections and so many people were defending and supporting Trump because he was 'standing up to China'', standing up to NATO', 'stopping immigrants', 'anti-Muslims', which warmed people's hearts.

The fact that he paid less tax than the average American worker, had a string of illicit extra marital affairs, thought that "grabbing women by the p..sy" was cool, was constantly pushing lies like that Obama was not born in the United States, thought that COVID was a joke etc. etc., was secondary.

Trump's blatant efforts to subvert and undermine the 2020 election results, continues to reflect the nature of the man. However, there is a deeper and scarier consequence to believing the propaganda and excusing this kind of behaviour. American democracy is being challenged today, and as such, democracy itself is being challenged.

When we allow propaganda, or a version of things that is closer to what we would like to believe, rather than the truth itself, to determine our choices, we are lost. When we choose leaders that pander to our narrow interests rather than the interests of the whole, we are lost.

We face a world today where democracy is not only being challenged from within the USA, but from without as well, from an inexorably rising behemoth that is China. China is the antithesis of democracy. It is a manifestation of the subjugation of the truth for the 'higher principles' of power and wealth, and of course, nationalism.

China is recovering what 'belongs to it', including Macau and Hong Kong, and Taiwan is next. Does it matter if the will of an independent nation and 24 million people are crushed? Does it matter if geopolitical stability and a global conflict is started and possibly thousands, if not millions of people are killed?

Russia played a part in the 2020 Election to help propagate some of Trump's lies, like the leaking of Hilary Clinton's emails. Russia has invaded and annexed Crimea in the face of international condemnation, and now Russia has invaded Ukraine. Thousands of young Russian soldiers are dying. Thousands of innocent Ukrainians are dying. There is untold suffering and spillovers as thousands flee into neighboring countries. Putin is the classic megalomaniac bully causing mayhem, and like all these successful bullies past and present, he has an ability to manipulate popular support through nationalistic propaganda.

Need we mention all the examples of the past, including two world wars?

I wish it was not such a romantic aspiration that we individually and collectively, as humans, determine the truth, and exercise our free will to make responsible choices, starting with ourselves. This includes selecting leaders for the right reasons. Leaders should make decisions on our behalf for our collective interest.

My attention falls to my own developing country and the deep sense of frustration I feel at the lost opportunities and unnecessary suffering our people endure because of leadership that repeats the mistakes of the past.

Papua New Guinea is blessed with all the natural endowments one could ask for and a relatively small population. We have wonderful bilateral and multilateral partners who are only too willing to help us. It has been 47 years since we gained independence in 1975, and yet we languish at the bottom of the United Nations Human Development Index.

When I became the National Planning Minister in 2012, we undertook to review the planning process from a governmental perspective, which led to the publication of the National Strategy for Responsible Sustainable Development (StaRS), the Medium Term Development Plan 2 (MTDP2), and the *National Planning and Responsibility Act 2016.*

The essence of StaRS was to examine our core beliefs as a people and a nation, make a truthful assessment of global, historical development experience, examine our own path to date, assess our circumstances and strengths, and ensure we were taking a **truly strategic and responsible development approach.** We also had to have a **process and structure to help ensure this.**

The StaRS recommended three frameworks; A Planning Framework, A Service Delivery Framework and A Monitoring and Evaluation Framework.

The **Planning Framework** should be guided by an overarching strategy (StaRS) and principles, and translate into successive five-year action plans (MTDPs), that **coincide with the five-year political cycle.** This way, there would be political support for the action plans. **This planning function should be in the custody of the Prime Minister himself and his department, not a Minister.**

The MTDP 2, that came after StaRS, only had a two-year life span from 2016 to 2017. This was to ensure that the incoming government after the 2017 Elections would publish a full five-year plan, MTDP 3, to cover that term of parliament – 2017 to 2022. Previous MTDPs concluded mid-term, meaning that an incoming government was inheriting the plan of a previous government and may have differing priorities.

StaRS recommended that, as a basis of a **Monitoring and Evaluation Framework,** there should be a separate ministry to focus on information, statistics, and monitoring. This should combine the National Statistics Office, National Identity and Civil Registry Office, and the monitoring functions of the Department of National Planning, into a Bureau of Statistics, to provide feedback and accountability into the process against the development plans and international reporting benchmarks.

The third framework that was developed was a **National Service Delivery Framework,** to establish the service delivery network, service delivery centres, minimum service levels and standards, and which levels of government that were responsible for providing which particular services.

These frameworks were all to be captured into an Act or Law which ultimately became the *National Planning and Responsibility Act,* which I tabled in Parliament in 2016.

We also drove a national publicity campaign called "PNG em Mi Yah!" (I am PNG). Change always started at an individual level. We were encouraging all Papua New Guineans to adopt and actually live the principles of responsible, sustainable development. We selected and promoted individuals as 'champions of StaRS' in different sectors.

At all times, everything we do must spring from our underlying beliefs, be they cultural or religious, or a combination of both. Papua New Guinea has a beautiful *Constitution*, and in it we subscribe to 'Papua New Guinea Ways' and our adopted Christian principles.

In 2009, I was the Culture and Tourism Minister in the Somare/Temu government. The Prime Minister had initiated a similar process to develop a "Vision 2050" under the auspices of Sir Puka Temu, who was the Deputy Prime Minister.

Submissions were called for from the public towards the consultations for the Vision 2050. I wrote a six-page letter dated the **19th June 2009**, titled, **"CALL FOR A PARADIGM SHIFT."**

This is an extract from that letter;

"..we must question the very development paradigm that we have adopted, by default, since independence, if we are to be truly strategic in our thinking.

We are led to believe that we must build a populous, growth driven, demand-based economy that keeps us under pressure to keep selling off resources and beholden to the foreign companies that we need to extract those resources. We are silly enough to just assume that we have to dance to that tune. It is that dance that is destroying the planet through climate change and it is that dance that is allowing our country to be stripped bare for the benefit of a small elite in the politico/ bureaucracy and large business.

..We need to realize that there are aspects of our own traditional culture relating to respect for the environment and communal well-being that are superior to that of the greed, self-centered cultural foundations of the Western model, and call on these.

This Vision will be grounded on such facts as the failure of the current policy, our comparative disadvantage in conducting a capitalist economy (a micro-example of this is the ability of Asians in running small business better than locals) because it is new to us and rather contrary to our traditional culture, our comparative advantage in terms of having a largely intact resource/ environment base, the implications of climate change, and our still relatively small population, and our ability to understand these tactical positions and plan around them."

In January of 2014, I wrote this as part of the Preamble to the StaRs;

"It has always been my view, as presented to the Vision 2050 committee in 2009, that we have not taken a TRULY STRATEGIC approach to these plans resulting in documents which are good but actually very generic in nature, which has resulted in operational plans which are also quite

standard. These plans could apply to any developing country. The only real country specific reference at a macro level is the PNG LNG project.

The doctrine of strategic planning requires that long-term plans begin at as high a vantage level as possible. AS SUCH, THEY SHOULD ACTUALLY BEGIN BY EXAMINING THE VERY DEVELOPMENT PARADIGM ITSELF - the underlying values and belief system that underpin the model. They must be strategic, leading to operational plans that quite specifically speak to our particular strengths and weaknesses, and seek to better position ourselves, based on these in a rapidly changing world.

To adopt a more strategic approach in our long-term planning we must first begin by examining the landscape before us in terms of historical experience.

Historical experience has led to a generally accepted model of an open market, demand driven, growth-based paradigm. This has resulted in a massive explosion of the human population and an equivalent huge appetite in terms of resources to sustain it. It has resulted in permanent and ongoing damage to the bio-systems of planet Earth, with frightening effects such as erratic and violent weather patterns and rising sea levels.

When we look at the world, we see an obvious rise in consciousness and concern about the impact of the human footprint on the planet. The incidences of global warming and climate change has alerted us to something we already knew, but tried to ignore - that the world is finite and cannot sustain endless growth. We see a shift in the value placed on the natural environment and a renewed emphasis on sustainable and responsible development. A physical examination of ourselves as a nation finds a country blessed with natural endowments and a relatively small, although rapidly growing, population.

We need to step back from this prevailing landscape and question the underlying paradigm and value system that is driving it. It is an oversimplification, but a truth that the current development process is driven very much by a values system based on individual interest and rights, the accumulation of wealth for self. More and bigger is better. It is predicated that an open market system will best allocate resources and drive development, that endless growth is a prerequisite for 'development'.

If we examine our Constitution we find a reference to PNG ways - a reference to the ways of our forefathers. This is a reference to a culture based on the sharing of wealth, community wellbeing rather than individual wellbeing and spiritual oneness with nature. This theme is found in many ancient cultures such as that of the American Indians. Similar values are at the heart of the Christian religion. This should help to lead the way back to a new paradigm.

We must question our automatic adoption of a paradigm that is quite contrary to this, particularly in the light of historical experience and a current new consciousness.

There are consequential changes happening to the planet that is forcing a revision of our development thinking and models, and we need to recognize this and help to lead the way back to a new paradigm.

These changes that represent part of the landscape before us are happening, whether we like it or not. A strategic planning process must take them into account.

As we attempt to strategically peer into the future, we should see a very different world. One where much greater emphasis and VALUE is placed on those factors that are the basis of a SUSTAINABLE and RESPONSIBLE economic modality, based on a value system more attuned to our ancient culture and Christian principles.

RESPONSIBLE DEVELOPMENT MEANS THAT WE DON'T UNDERTAKE ACTIVITIES WHICH COMPROMISE THE WORLD'S BIODIVERSITY OR PUTS OUR CHILDRENS' FUTURE AT RISK. SUSTAINABILITY IS A CATEGORY OF RESPONSIBLE DEVELOPMENT AND MEANS THAT WE DEVELOP AN ECONOMY WHICH PROVIDES ALL OF THE ELEMENTS FOR THE WELL-BEING OF OUR CITIZENS IN A MANNER THAT IS SELF-PERPETUATING.

With these principles in mind, we set about the next level of the strategic plan.

What are our strategic strengths or strategic assets in this new context? In the 'new world', the greatest value will be placed on these assets that contribute to sustainable food and water security, sustainable energy, and mitigate the effects of climate change.

In our country, this would point generally to our relatively intact environment and large biodiversity, but more specifically, to our forests which contain the third largest remaining rainforest in the world, our tuna stocks which make up 15 percent of the world's tuna stocks, and together with the Parties to the Nauru Agreement, make up 30 percent of the world's tuna stocks, our hydro and geothermal potentials as well as gas reserves, our fertile land, clean and abundant water, and agricultural background.

Our current development plans and pathway are actually eroding these assets. By pursuing this accepted development pathway, we are actually caught in a cycle of demand (an ever-growing population demanding services), profits, and growth-driven policies, that are resulting in actions that rely heavily on easier means of satisfying this demand, such as primary resources extraction. This is undermining our long-term assets and economy.

It also results in activities that are reactions to symptoms such as poverty and crime, rather than addressing underlying causalities, such as population growth, because population growth is an integral part of the old paradigm.

The difficulty in our planning strategy is how to begin to move out of this cycle before we find ourselves with a massive population with an equal appetite and a severely depleted and damaged environment. It is difficult because we are challenged everyday with the primary and symptomatic issues of education, health, law and order, and keeping the economy steaming along to generate the revenues required to meet these needs. It will require a staged approach, but must be very deliberate. Our current plans do not provide for this clarity.

The number of human beings in any given limited space is a fundamental driver of need. Rather than seeing this as a desirable aspect of a progressive economy, it should be recognized as an underlying contributor to the development problem. Ever-increasing numbers of people require resources to service them and places pressure on the Government to pursue unsustainable policies. Having valuable mineral and petroleum resources has meant that our country has deferred learning hard lessons.

The strategic assets, together with a stabilized population growth rate give us the basic variables for a responsible and sustainable economy - one that can feed and energize itself and export surplus to generate foreign exchange to pay for our import needs.

We must redesign our policies around the strategic assets of fisheries, particularly skipjack tuna, forestry, and water. These are globally significant assets because of their quantum and because they provide a solution to sustainable food and water security and climate change (carbon sink and oxygen production), energy, and a biodiversity reservoir. *The strategic partnerships of Parties to The Nauru Agreement, for tuna, and the Coalition of Rainforest Nations, for the forests, are crucial.*

We need to examine the nature of our soil and weather and undertake to encourage the growth of only agricultural produce that we can grow competitively. Are we able to produce grain crops, such as rice and wheat, on a large-scale, competitively, for example? Or do they require long-term subsidization. Perhaps we are better off pursuing large-scale root crop production and sago, and the importation of rice? The high rainfall in most areas of the country provides for numerous rivers, all with good volume and flow rates. These can provide both a source of clean, sustainable power, water for export, and carbon credits. A single dam on the Purari River, for example, can provide for five times the required on-and-off grid current power requirement for the country.

The intact environment also provides the basis of a FUTURE ECONOMY, based on our strategic assets of tourism, medical research, green technology and carbon credits, etc. An important factor of this future economy is the foreign capital that we can attract to build this economy because of our opportunity cost and the desire of the world to encourage such action. By revising our development road-map we can actively pursue international aid and commercial funding to contribute to a fund to compensate for opportunity cost as well as investments in global solutions through a new economy.

PNG can be seen to be a world leader in a world looking for solutions through such forums as the Coalition of Rainforest Nations, and Parties to the Nauru Agreement, rather than an impoverished nation always playing catch-up. A marketing strategy can be conducted in conjunction with the New Economy Fund to reposition PNG in the eyes of the world.

If we continue doing as the current Development Strategic Plan (DSP 2030) suggests, we will have a population of 30 million by 2050, surviving on an economy heavily based on the extractive industries sector and an environment badly damaged by this, and forest and tuna stocks greatly depleted by unsustainable harvesting. Even if we begin a population stabilization program tomorrow, at the current demographic profile the numbers will reach 24 million before it stabilizes. We will have become an example on a large scale of what has happened on Kiriwina and Karkar Islands. We must begin a strategic and deliberate intervention now.

Changing the development paradigm will have to be staged because of the prevalence and immediacy of our goods and services deficit. There will have to be a calculated environmental and philosophical compromise in the short and medium terms.

Intermediate plans therefore will have to rely on 'old economy' developments to sustain current needs and lay the infrastructure, education, and health foundations while the population is stabilized and investment begun around our strategic assets and future economy. This can be structured around the current gas project.

A policy examining the staging and general approach to further large-scale extractive projects needs to be developed immediately. The establishment of a Sovereign Wealth Fund from current mineral and gas proceeds for the provision of an income stream into the future is required.

The National Strategy for Responsible Sustainable Development (StaRS), offers a new development paradigm. It builds on the gains made by the Vision 2050 and the current DSP 2030 and prescribes a new development road-map that incorporates these elements which make for a growth strategy that is truly strategic, futuristic and appropriate for the future.

This new development strategy will be reflected in successive MTDPs and will be supported by the newly adopted National Monitoring and Evaluation Framework, which provides for the tracking and reporting of progress on goals and envisioned outcomes.

As the Minister for National Planning and Monitoring, I commend this new development strategy and urge the nation to truly respond and embrace the call for a paradigm shift in mindset and expectations for the future for this generation as well as the next.

By embracing the call for a change in paradigm we will be able to recognize the meaning of PNG WAYS and be truly STRATEGIC in our understanding of the context of HISTORICAL EXPERIENCE and the strategic positioning of our country in the NEW WORLD CONSCIOUSNESS AND ORDER.

Accordingly, it is with great pleasure and hope that I commend the National Strategy for Responsible Sustainable Development to the nation and the people of Papua New Guinea.

Submission to the Vision 2050 consultations by Hon. Charles Abel, Minister for Culture and Tourism, 19th June 2009

National Strategy for Responsible Sustainable Development (StaRS)

Chapter 19

Eight Days

"PNG's FIRST BOND ISSUE RECEIVES TOP REVIEW" - Leading financial news and data publication, Global Capital Asia, has just named Papua New Guinea's debut US$500 million (K1.7 billion) bond issue as the best sovereign bond issue for 2018. This comes on the back of Finance Asia's achievement award for excellence in 2018, and The Asset's country awards best bond and best syndicated loan for 2018. **(The National, 14 December 2018).**

"Excuse me Deputy Prime Minister, but where exactly is New Guinea again?"

I took a deep breath. This was perhaps the 30th meeting of this whirlwind trip. I would open up the floor for questions, bracing myself for all of the financial and technical queries, but I'd often had this same question.

"Please note that our country is Papua New Guinea, not New Guinea. If you have an idea where Australia is in the Western Pacific, PNG is just north of Australia. Thank you."

It was in New York, at the Lotte New York Palace Hotel, 455 Madison Avenue, in the Garrison Room on the 5th Floor.

Papua New Guinea was hosting a lunch for a room full of potential investors comprising representatives from all of the major banks and investor funds including, Apollo Global Management, Van Eck Associates, Nomura Asset Management, Columbia Finance, HSBC Bank, TIAA Bank, Stone Harbour Investment Partners, Ashmore Group, and Cerberus Capital Management.

They were considering the first-ever commercial sovereign debt placement from this small Pacific country.

I had taken the podium once again as Deputy Prime Minister, Treasurer, and host, heading a team, together with the Treasury Secretary, Dairi Vele, and the Central Bank Governor, Loi Bakani, to promote Papua New Guinea's inaugural sovereign bond issue.

It was the first time for our nation to stand before cold blooded international investors and offer a financial instrument in the global market, based on competitive financial terms.

This was not going to the International Monetary Fund, World Bank or bilateral friends such Australia, with cap in hand as a developing nation begging for help.

PNG was finally taking this massive step to expose itself to the discipline of the real marketplace on its own feet, and raise financing like a truly independent nation.

Despite claiming political independence in 1975, Papua New Guinea has, by and large, remained financially dependent on its multilateral and bilateral development partners.

Annual budgets have had to be supported through deficit financing and grant aid from the outset. Apart from the domestic funding component through government-issued debt instruments, the foreign sourced financing has been almost totally concessional. It has come from institutions such the World Bank and the Asian Development Bank which were established and funded by the developed nations to support lesser developed, and developing nations.

External debt, as at 31st December 2017 was K6 385 million. This represented 8.6 percent of Gross Domestic Product. Some 84.9 percent of this debt stock was from multilateral and bilateral creditors, such as the Asian Development Bank, Japan International Cooperation Agency, Export Import Bank of China, and the World Bank. Total debt, as a percentage of Gross Domestic Product was 31.2 percent. (As I write this in December 2022 debt to GDP is now close to 60 percent).

This financing comes with requirements, such as an extraordinary procurement process, project rather than budget financing, specific sector interventions, the use of source country contractors, and structural reforms. These requirements are arguably in the interest of the recipient although there are examples, such as the IMF prescriptive structural reforms of the 1990s, that proved to be very problematic for many countries, including PNG.

The PNG Department of Treasury has aspired for some time to begin a journey into the commercial debt market through a sovereign bond issuance. This would make available a ready form of financing that could be tapped as needed, and at improved rates as a reputation was established. It would also begin to wean PNG off of the dependence on concessional financing and aid.

Treasury had actually made three failed attempts over two decades. The most recent attempt was the aborted bid in 2016 because of the subdued global economy, low commodity prices, El Nino drought effects in PNG, uncertainty over LNG plant production levels, and the elevated risk in global financial markets.

"They previously found the market was not responsive," says Paul Barker, Executive Director of the Institute of National Affairs.

It was always going to be a rigorous and daunting exercise and I had no illusions, as the incoming Treasurer in 2017, as to this challenge that had never been undertaken by PNG. To add to our challenges, we had the massive earthquake on the 26th of

February 2018 which disrupted the PNG LNG production and resulted in a country credit rating downgrade for PNG.

PNG was basically unknown in the international market, and when it was examined these all too familiar risks were exposed;

- Narrow export base;
- Exposure to the commodity cycle;
- Inability to reduce budget deficits;
- Lack of adequate infrastructure to accelerate economic growth;
- Limited exchange rate flexibility;
- Inability to fully benefit from the portion of international reserves held in offshore accounts;
- Inability to cope with negative global economic and business conditions;
- Inability to implement key economic and social reforms;
- Reliance on the operations of the PNG LNG project and other major mines;
- Natural disasters (Pacific Ring of Fire) such as the 2015 drought impact on Ok Tedi, and agriculture, and the Hela earthquake 2018;
- Inability to establish the Sovereign Wealth Fund;
- Infrequent statistics;
- Actual or perceived instances of money laundering;
- Political and social developments;
- Foreign exchange demand backlog;
- Unfunded pension liabilities;
- Human rights issues, gender based violence, police brutality;
- Security risks and the effect on cost of business;
- Land use and land ownership issues;
- Substantial fluctuations in exchange rates against the US dollar could affect repayments;
- Rise in overseas interest rates;
- Future inability to obtain financing may affect ability to meet payments on public debt;
- Any downgrade on PNG's sovereign rating could affect market value and the tradability of the notes;
- No established market yet for these notes, hence trading value is uncertain; and
- Non-enforcement of foreign judgements may limit the ability of holders to recover damages from the issuer.

Nevertheless, within a comprehensive strategy to rebuild revenue, renegotiate the Porgera Mine agreement, progress the Papua LNG and Wafi Golpu resource projects, and restructure debt away from expensive short-term domestic borrowing, as initiated under the 100 Day Plan, we took the bull by its sharp horns. We had eight years of political stability behind us and had successfully delivered the world class PNG LNG

Project with ExxonMobil and other global companies. With the prospect of the PNG LNG coming off its debt in 2024 and the pending 'three train' construction activity pipeline from the Papua LNG, and P'nyang project, we had an excellent story to tell.

With the Deputy Prime Minister and Treasurer at the forefront, and a very articulate Treasury Secretary in Dairi Vele, and knowledgeable Governor for the Bank of PNG in Loi Bakani, we made a formidable presentation team.

"Specifically, a US dollar bond by PNG will be a critical milestone for the country as it serves as the first publicly traded security on an international platform, allowing PNG to diversify its source of funding and establish a benchmark for the country's future budget requirements. More importantly, raising these external US dollar funds will shift PNG's borrowings from the high cost and saturated domestic market, and provide much needed duration (target bond is 5 and/or 10 years), which would relieve ratings agencies pressure." ***(briefing note from Secretary Treasurer to Treasurer, 21st August 2018).***

It was not the intention to pretend to suddenly abandon concessional financing and the established sources of funding, including grant funding. These would remain the primary avenues for the foreseeable future. In fact, as part of the 100 Day Plan we committed to and launched the **world's first Medium Term Revenue Strategy**, and committed to a staffing program with the World Bank in conjunction with this strategy.

To rebuild the Highlands Highway, we committed to a multi-tranche funding package of one billion US dollars from the Asian Development Bank.

The sovereign bond was a small stepping stone in overall financial terms, but a huge step for our country towards economic maturity.

In the shorter term, it was a part of the Treasury's Medium Term Debt Strategy 2018 – 2022, to diversify away from an over-reliance on the short-term domestic money market which had rates at 12 percent at the time and rising, lengthen the maturity profile, open up an alternate source of funding and bring in much needed foreign exchange. The funding from the bond was also a key feature of the 2018 Budget, as approved by Parliament in November 2017.

The government's reliance on short-term debt was one of the key issues flagged by Moody's international rating agency, when it put PNG's credit on a negative outlook in March 2018.

In Chapter 10, I described the state of absolute exhaustion I was in on the last leg of an ***eight days*** around the world trip we had just completed. We had conducted some sixty conferences, interviews and press conferences in six major financial centres of the world, working during the day and flying at night through all possible time zones. We had engaged with over 100 potential investors during this time. Believe it or not, I had also maintained my daily exercise program, often attending the gym at 2 a.m. or 3 a.m. in the morning. My body had had enough. My heart was beating all over the place, and I was having difficulty breathing on the final flight home through Nandi and Honiara.

It was 'D-Day', 28th September 2018. This was the name used for the June 6th 1944 Allied invasion of the beaches of Normandy on the French coast to repel the Nazis, during the Second World War. It signifies 'the day of reckoning!'

The bond had to be launched with the opening of the New York stock exchange, and priced (interest rate) based on preliminary bids received. If this pricing was within the Cabinet approved price range, the Prime Minister was required to give his approval as a formality. Then the bond had to be sold into an order book for at least 500 million US dollars. This had to take place between 8 a.m. to 3 p.m. New York time (10 p.m. to 5 a.m. PNG time). Cabinet had to be on standby in case the pricing had to be revised above nine percent.

The roadshow had been from the 3rd to the 12th of September covering Singapore, Hong Kong, London, New York, Boston, and Los Angeles.

The market had shown a preference for a 10-year bond, rather than five years to match our LNG production outlook, with a minimum $500 million tranche to qualify for the secondary market. The secondary market means that the bond can be traded at any time after it is purchased. This configuration of amount and duration is what we had gone with.

At 10 p.m. PNG time and 8 a.m. New York time, we announced the transaction into the US market. As our book-runners built up the order book and price offers we needed the Prime Minister to sign off on the final price guidance by 10:15 a.m. New York time (12:15 a.m. PNG time). This was assuming that the pricing remained below the Cabinet approved nine percent ceiling.

It was 1:30 a.m. at night in Port Moresby as I clung to the phone with Prime Minister O'Neill on one line, and our brokers on another. We were all under tremendous pressure, not knowing if there would be any significant real uptake of the bond, and at what actual price. We had seen some interest in the lead up following the roadshow and in a tentative order book, but could not be sure until the market actually opened.

Significant cost and effort had gone into the exercise, and for PNG to fail, or withdraw for a fourth time, would be a disaster.

As the team leader, I had a lot of political pressure on me as well with the usual 'naysayers' and criticism.

The orders came in very slowly at first. Very small parcels by lesser-known investors. The pressure built and built. I began to despair as the clock ticked towards the 11:30

a.m. New York deadline for the Prime Minister to sign off on the final pricing and volume.

Then like a godsend I heard the brokers excited voice,

"Goldmans has placed an order for a 100 m!"

The floodgates opened. By 11:30 a.m. New York time, we had received orders for US$3.8 billion. I now came under tremendous pressure from the brokers to increase our placement.

I refused, choosing to stick to the US$500 million. We needed to show the world we were not desperate, and were determined to show discipline and build our brand in the market, over time.

The pricing was at 8.375 percent, at the lower end of the expectations from our advisors and the market.

We had 215 separate orders and the final book ended up with 125 different investors led by Goldman Sachs, Stone Harbour Investment Partners, Wellington Management Company, and Aberdeen Asset Managers.

Interestingly, US accounts ended up with a 56 percent allocation, while European investors took 27 percent and Asia just 17 percent. The majority of the trade – 93 percent was allocated to fund managers.

"Global Capital Asia, Capital Markets Awards 2018: Bonds, 11 December 2018"

BEST SSA (SOVEREIGN) BOND

The Independent State of Papua New Guinea's $500m debut bond

Global Coordinator: Credit Suisse

Bookrunner and lead manager: Citi

It was a deal nobody thought would get done, and with good reason. PNG's inaugural bond was decades in the making. After multiple mandates and roadshows, it seemed like every debt banker in Asia had worked on the sovereign's potential bond sale at some point in their careers. So, when the frontier market nation decided to venture out to the market, yet again this year, it was almost a case of the boy who cried wolf. It seemed impossible that a B2/B rated country could successfully pull off a deal in late September, amid a particularly rough emerging market backdrop.

Yet, this time around, failure wasn't an option, and PNG's eventual feat at pulling off its maiden issuance is worthy of this award.

Kudos needs to go to the sovereign's smart approach with its fundraising. PNG started its 144A/Reg S transaction by speaking with investors about both a five and ten-year tenor. While Asian investors tended to favour the shorter maturity, PNG found that the accounts in the US liked the decade option.

Ultimately, PNG opted to pursue just the longer dated tranche, knowing it could play to the demand from large asset managers in the US with a benchmark sized transaction that would qualify for inclusion in emerging market indices.

It was vindicated with its strategy, as US investors drove the transaction, pushing orders to a peak of $3.8bn during book building. US accounts ended up with a 56% allocation, while European investors took 27% and Asia just 17%. The majority of the trade, 93% was allocated to fund managers.

PNG also showed its savvy in other ways. While the hefty book could have easily allowed for a larger transaction, PNG made the prudent choice of keeping its bond at US$500m so as not to put pressure on investors. The coupon and yield of 8.375% were also remarkable, considering the state of emerging markets at the time, and the frontier status of PNG itself. Even a banker away from the deal lauded its execution, as well as final completion.

For the banks working on the trade, pitching PNG as an attractive credit was an uphill battle, as many accounts were looking at the issuer for the first time. Like other frontier markets, the country is known for its fragile political situation and domestic instability. There was also an unusual spotlight on it this year, as PNG hosted the APEC summit in November.

Needless to say, the pressure was on for the government to prove itself to the world, while also appealing for investments to support its ambitious infrastructure plans. The bookrunners pitch of PNG offering diversity, and exposure to a new name in emerging markets, paid off.

While it may be unlikely that PNG will venture into the dollar market again in the near future, the sovereign's deal is nonetheless monumental. Its success opens up the possibility of future issuance from other PNG borrowers, something that was just a pipe dream before. This victory has created new dynamics for PNG, and helped draw the country into a new stage of economic development."

An extract from the bond roadshow program showing the New York day schedule, Monday 10th September 2018;

- ✓ 12:25 p.m. arrived from London - New York, to The Dominick Hotel 246 Spring Street, New York.
- ✓ 7:15 a.m. pick-up
- ✓ 8 a.m. Conference Call – INVESCO
- ✓ 9:30 a.m. Meeting with – NWI (NY based hedge fund manager), Marathon, Blue Mountain
- ✓ 11 a.m.; Meeting JPMIM (JP Morgan)
- ✓ 12:30 p.m.; Investor Lunch, Lotte New York Palace Hotel, 455 Madison Avenue

- ✓ 2 p.m.; Lazard (financial advisory firm)
- ✓ 3:30 p.m.; GSAM Goldman Sachs Asset Management
- ✓ 5 p.m.; Prudential Financial
- ✓ 8 p.m.; Depart New York for Boston

Charles K. Abel, press conference on arrival from the bond roadshow, September 2018.

Chapter 20

So Much Gold

"Papua New Guinea is a mountain of gold floating in a sea of oil."

How often do we hear that famous line from Sir Julius Chan repeated?

If you add to the mineral and petroleum wealth, the tuna, forestry, biodiversity, abundant water, and mild climate, you would surely be tempted to declare PNG as one of the most blessed countries in the world. I wrote more broadly on this in Chapter 18 **"Reaching for the Stars"**. However, here, I want to expound more specifically on the mineral and petroleum wealth factor.

"Mr. Prime Minister, I'm sorry to keep repeating this, but the way the Kumul companies are structured, particularly Kumul Petroleum and Kumul Minerals, effectively creates a 'cash trap'."

"By placing our equity in the hands of a company means that all of our dividends from any resource project will effectively pass through an intermediary that is governed by a board that only reports to the Prime Minister."

"Prime Minister, billions of Kina of public funds will be under the discretion of a board that may have a different agenda from that of Government. As Planning Minister, I don't have to remind Cabinet that we continue to run deficit budgets. We are not able to fund the development needs of our country. We need those dividend streams to come into the Treasury accounts to fund our number one money plan, which is the National Budget, as sanctioned by Parliament."

It was a National Executive Council meeting in early 2015 and the discussion was the purported Kumul group of companies, and in particular the vesting of all the State's shareholding in mineral and petroleum resource projects in Kumul Minerals and Kumul Petroleum.

"We need to establish a proper Sovereign Wealth Fund (SWF) governed by the Santiago Principles for SWFs, not a structure which does not report to Parliament and has too much discretion over massive amounts of public resources. My fellow Ministers, once you create this animal and breathe life into it – it will become very powerful, financially and politically."

The Pacific Ring of Fire is a horseshoe-shaped zone of intense seismic and volcanic activity around the Pacific Ocean.

With 75 percent of the earth's volcanoes and 90 percent of all earthquakes, the Pacific Ring of Fire is home to many rich mineral deposits, such as gold, copper, molybdenum, and other metals.

The Guardian Magazine's analysis reveals that "each year nearly 11 million tonnes of fuel and oil (the equivalent of 1 100 Eiffel Towers) are extracted from the region, 2 million tonnes of copper, nickel, manganese and aluminium are mined, and gold worth US$ 2.6 billion is quarried."

"But despite the minerals and wealth pulled from the Pacific's mountains, valleys, oceans, and rivers, communities often have little to show for it. But nowhere is the impact of mining – its booms and busts, potentials and pitfalls – felt more acutely than across Papua New Guinea's broad archipelago."

There have been small-scale gold rushes occurring in PNG since the 1870s. In the early chapters I described some of the issues my great grandfather had in protecting the people from the rough-handed tactics of miners as they suddenly invaded, 'en masse', parts of Milne Bay in search of the yellow metal in the first decade of the 20th Century.

Up until 1970, there was little commercial mineral extraction in Papua New Guinea. Since the 1970s, mineral extraction has dominated the national economy, and we have had the full ambit of historical experiences with the 'resource curse' from a painful civil war in Bouganville, to the wholesale destruction of the Fly River system from tailings sedimentation.

Oil and gas extraction were added to the party in the early 1990s.

The Extractive Industries Transparency Initiative 2020 Report emphasizes the domination of this sector in our economy;

In 2019, the extractive sector (oil, gas and minerals) contributed 28 percent of Gross Domestic Product (a financial measure of the value of total domestic production in a year), or K 24 billion.

In 2020, it was 26 percent of GDP, or K 22 billion.

Some 86 percent of total exports came from the extractive sector, of which 38 percent was Liquified Natural Gas (LNG), and 32 percent was gold.

In terms of revenue to the government – and this is where it gets tricky depending on the inclusion or exclusion of certain indirect revenue streams, such as dividends to state-owned authorities or corporations (which obviously should be included), in 2019, the extractive sector provided 28 percent of government revenue, and in 2020 it was 23 percent.

China, Australia, Russia, and Canada are, respectively, the largest producers of gold in the world, as of 2022. Global production of gold reached approximately 3 100 metric tonnes that year.

In 2022, PNG ranked 17th in the world in terms of gold production, producing 50 tonnes.

China was the highest with 330 tons and Australia second with 320 tonnes.

From the various gold projects, that I have listed in Addendum 1, historically from the 1970s to today, and looking to imminent projects, we have mined, or will mine in the near future, over three thousand tonnes of gold. The price of gold hit an historical high in 2020 of US$ 2 070 an ounce (we somehow managed to shut down one of our largest gold producers in the Porgera Mine in 2019, and it remains shut four years later).

If we value our gold production at a very conservative US$ 1 000 an ounce, we calculate a total production value of close to US$100 billion, or at US$ 0.28 to the Kina, today's exchange rate – K 357 billion.

It costs money to find and dig up, transport, and refine gold (of up to US$ 1 200 per ounce in today's terms). But, let's say we could design a fiscal regime where we took 25 percent of the gross revenue of gold alone. This would translate to K 89 billion, and at an historical average of K 10 billion per Annual Budget, would fully fund nine national budgets out of our 47 years of existence.

This is gold alone. We have silver, copper, nickel and cobalt. We have oil and gas, fisheries, forestry, and agriculture. We have an abundance of natural wealth and huge quantities of it are exported every year.

Under the current fiscal regime, since LNG production began in 2014, around 25 percent of our current National Budget comes from the extractive resource sector.

The first point though is to acknowledge that **significant resources in the billions of Kina have come to the government and its various arms, institutions, and to landowners, from the extractive sector.**

The second point is to question is **what is happening to this money?**

On the 2nd of December 2022, Exxon Mobil, the operator of the PNG LNG Project published the payments to Government up to October 2022 from this project since 2014;

- Kumul Petroleum K7.7 billion
- Taxes K7.3 billion
- MRDC (landowners) K1.4 billion
- Royalties K900 million
- Development Levies K700 million

These totalled up to K18 billion.

The third question is, how do we **improve the take to our country and the landowners, whilst minimizing environmental damage and negative social impacts?**

This take is not restricted to direct financial payments to the State, but includes other factors such as training and employment, local and landowner business participation, domestic energy security, supporting our foreign exchange requirements, infrastructure obligations, and how do we convert some of the monetary take into a sustainable future income stream through a **proper sovereign wealth or investment fund.**

I always come from the premise that the private sector knows best how to run business. As soon as the government gets involved it becomes political and inefficient.

The role of government is to create a conducive, competitive, and fair environment for business and then regulate, collect taxes, and invest into the socioeconomic requirements of its people.

It is not the role of government to run commercial businesses, unless it is to provide an essential service that the private sector cannot.

We have a choice amongst most of the best global companies in the extractive industry as to whom to partner with. They have the expertise and capital to explore and develop the resources, when found, in the most efficient manner. If a Papua New Guinean company should emerge one day from the private sector to compete, well and good. Otherwise, the presumption is we have to work with an international partner.

When I testified at the Commission of Inquiry into the UBS loan on the 30th of July 2021, I explained that the pursuit of expensive debt to take up our equity rights in the exploitation of our own resources is wrong and unnecessary.

I said, that we are the State, not a private sector participant. We don't have to assume the same risks, including the funding risk, as such.

Our laws are good, in the sense that we get an automatic equity participation right in the event of a resource being discovered, and the project moving to development stage. We don't participate in the exploration risk as a result. However, we still need to find the capital to buy our shares. The rationale for this is so that we can better participate in returns from a project.

When I led the negotiations on the Papua LNG Project, we introduced a number of progressions on the PNG LNG Project.

One of them was 'carried financing', where the investor would arrange our financing for us on the same terms they were getting, for our back in rights.

We also doubled the royalty rate, made no concessions on corporate income tax, introduced a domestic gas supply obligation at a fixed price, required a mandatory local content plan, an onshore minimum foreign currency holding, and third-party access to the gas pipeline. In my view, we began **a progression towards less reliance on equity and more on a taxation and royalty based fiscal regime.**

We were able to access consultants who were paid for by the World Bank, and by the Australian Government, as well as a team from our Treasury Department.

We were able to obtain 51 percent of the net free cashflow from the project based on the open book modelling that was used by both parties, and vetted by the smart people who were helping us.

I note in recent times the renegotiation of the Porgera Gold Mine project, effectively shutting the mine down for four years, and initially asking for 100 percent ownership. We then gradually backed down to 51 percent equity and are claiming 61 percent of the take under the new terms. In order to increase our stake to 51 per cent we have to purchase an additional 31 percent. This capital cost plus our corresponding share of the mine reopening costs will be deducted from our share of the proceeds from the reopened mine.

When I was Treasurer, we had already put to Barrick, the owner, a position of 15 percent additional free carried equity, and a 10 percent royalty (an increase of 8 percent). This gave PNG a 57% take of the net free cash flow at **no extra cost to the State**. Further, it did not involve shutting the mine indefinitely, with all the loss of employment, revenue, start-up costs, and impact on our international credibility.

I've said on numerous occasions, including at the UBS Inquiry, that – EQUITY IS OVERATED, particularly if you are the State.

Some level of free equity should be factored into the fiscal mix to give visibility to the operation, but the fiscal tools to be used are a production based, market price-based royalty, corporate income tax, and possibly an additional profit tax. These should be factored around a declared take, that is calculated by the expert help as the maximum possible, given the particulars of the discovery. It may be easily accessible with low landowner density, for example, enabling a lower cost structure and higher possible take to the State.

This sort of regime is much **cheaper, easier to implement and monitor, and provides earlier cashflows to the State**. It eliminates such expensive and unnecessary distractions such as the IPIC loan for the PNG LNG Project (and subsequently the UBS loan transaction), because we don't have to find the capital to buy our shares, like every other investor.

The next matter is ensuring that these huge revenue returns are passed through Treasury, and a proportion spills into a Santiago principled SWF. There are numerous successful examples around the world of this regime.

Currently, we don't have this. We spend huge amounts of money through borrowings to buy our shares and wait for the debt to be repaid. Then any dividends we do receive are placed into a company where we know little about what happens to the funds, or the funds are expended on lower priorities. In the meantime, our budgets are inadequate, heavily debt financed, and our debt-to-GDP ratio is at a record level.

(Note, Addendum 1; Papua New Guinea Mineral and Petroleum Resource Projects Summary, and Addendum 2; The Santiago Principles.)

Sir Julius Chan and Sir Michael Somare, September 2020.

Chapter 21

It Does Not Belong to You

When Jacinda Arden announced her resignation as New Zealand Prime Minister on the 19th of January 2023, I posted on social media, **"In other countries, they know when to let it go."**

Scotland's First Minister, Nicola Sturgeon, announced her resignation on the 15th of February 2023. She said, "I know that as time passed, I would have less and less energy to give to the job. And I can't do the job on anything other than a 100 percent basis. The country deserves nothing less than that."

These were successful, long-term Parliamentarians who resigned, not out of any particular controversy, but in the best interests of the country, when they felt that they could not continue to give their all.

When I went into my last election in 2022, I did so, knowing full well that I was leaving my relatively safe seat of Alotau Open, to contest the more difficult challenge of the Regional Seat for Milne Bay. No election is easy and I was facing some challenges at home because of my tough stance on law and order. Nevertheless, it was obvious that I was taking a greater risk in the bigger seat.

I explained at great length to the people in every council ward that I visited, that one of the responsibilities of a leader is to prepare the way for the future. This is not easy as it means contemplating the prospect of making yourself redundant. However, a leader should think first of the well-being of those for whom he/she is responsible.

The trappings of leadership are very alluring for obvious reasons, and I often joke about how a person who fortuitously emerges the winner from the great raffle that is a PNG election, and begins a metamorphosis into a 'leader' with the requisite enlarges abdomen, multiple wives, and multiple controversies. The majority will lose the following election, and spend the rest of their days trying to get back into Parliament. A select few, on the other hand, never seem to lose no matter what!

I don't think anyone has ever voluntarily relinquished leadership in our country. When it comes to a sitting MP not recontesting, for reasons other than health, I can only think of three politicians, and one of them was Cecil Abel in 1972.

The example of Nelson Mandela stands in stark contrast to many other leaders from his continent. He was jailed for twenty-seven years for standing up for the rights of his people. When finally released, and he ultimately became South Africa's first President voted in a fully representative democratic election, and first black Head of State, he was not vindictive over his experience. Mandela, despite his standing and sacrifice, only served one term. He actually declined a second term and was succeeded by his Deputy. His example is an exception, not the rule.

A leader in any position holds that position in a trustee capacity only, on behalf others. The position **does not belong to you**.

In all my speeches to the people of Alotau, and Milne Bay, I explained that I had been blessed to serve them and the country for three terms, but it was time to allow other leaders to emerge. I had been grooming several leaders for this purpose, and I presented those leaders to them. These included a current Local-Level Government President (who went on to win the seat), the former District Administrator, and the former Women's Representative in the Alotau District Development Authority.

My role as a leader was to represent them as best I could as their voice in Parliament, and their advocate for improved government services. Just as importantly I had to set a good example in my personal life and conduct, as an honest and principled leader.

An aspect of this example was also to prepare and allow the transition of power. When a leader takes this mindset, he is more apt to play that custodian role, establish systems that don't overly rely on him, and not get too emotionally attached to the trappings of power.

Conversely, a leader can become obsessed with retaining power, and that becomes the focus, rather than the purpose for which he or she was elected in the first place. **A true leader is willing to make sacrifices, and promote other leaders**.

I was also presenting my people with the option of supporting a Party with a leader from their own province, in Our Development Party - the Party founded by Sir Puka Temu.

As their leader, I had to present to them options for the future. I was not just abandoning them. I had been all the way to Deputy Prime Minister, Minister for Treasury, Minister for Planning, and Minister for Finance. I had delivered on a local level beyond any previous Member. I was now a party leader and presented a platform based on FAITH, FAMILY, TEAMWORK, and ACTION, which are all principles that I had tried my best to exemplify.

I lost the regional race in the 2022 General Elections, but had total peace in my heart knowing that I had taken all possible steps to be a good example, set a path for future leaders, and present options for my people.

The Lord had blessed me with yet another opportunity in life, and I dropped everything and put 110 percent of myself into it.

My dear father's health took a turn for the worse during the election, and following my loss, I was able to spend the last months of his life at his bedside, including living in the hospital with him for a month. I had a role to fulfil as a son as well. I made sure my dad knew how grateful I was for his life and how much I loved him.

On the point of leadership transition - it must always be based on an institutionalized process that is based on competency and nothing else.

There is a sense of unearned entitlement that can be very dangerous for individuals and organizations. In some ways, it can be like the pitfalls of the inheritance of wealth in a family situation. Entitlements that are unearned often lead to dysfunction, abuse, and waste. **Power structures sustained artificially rather than on the basis of competency lead to tyranny.**

In my Church, the Kwato Church, I am the great grandson of the founder, the Reverend Charles William Abel. This only, possibly, qualifies me as a member of the congregation. In no way does it entitle me to any other position or authority in the Church.

I am a three-term Member of Parliament for Alotau Open. This does not entitle me to remain there for life, or to expect to do so. Once again, it is not about the individual, it is about the people and the organization. A good leader is the first to recognize this and act accordingly. A good leader keeps his pride and ego in check.

Leadership is not confined to Parliament. It is required at all levels. In all cases A LEADER LEADS BY EXAMPLE. It is also the minimum that we must demand of our leaders.

"A leader is one who knows the way, goes the way, and shows the way. The greatest leadership is by example. You must do, act, say, and be the person you want your team to be." **(John Maxwell, 10th May 2019).**

Words without corresponding action, especially from a leader are empty and carry no weight.

A leader is faithful to his word and to his people. He or she demonstrates these principles, starting with himself and his or her family. **If a leader cannot be faithful to his or her spouse, if a leader cannot be faithful to his or her family, how can they be faithful to you?**

If a leader professes to be a Christian but breaks this commitment to the Lord every day, how can he or she be committed to you?

If we, as members of the Church support such leaders, how are we being faithful to the Word? How do we then expect such leaders to perform in their role as leaders, and why are we so often disappointed in their performance?

When I am listening to the powerful words of a preacher, politician, businessman, or indeed anyone who is trying to convey a message, I want to see some evidence that they have lived it and can demonstrate the outcomes.

Any person in a position of influence or leadership, which I believe is nearly everyone in some capacity, must add value. This begins with taking responsibility for yourself, and then for those who may depend on you. You cannot add value if you cannot even sustain yourself independently, or have no discipline in your life.

Jesus was the ultimate example of service and sacrifice. He preached about right living, and moved and performed miracles. He took on human form and suffered the anguish of the knowledge of what was required of him from his Father. He faced the pain and humility of death on the cross and endured it, not because of any fault of his own, but for the sake of others. Is this not the example of leadership in action?

My great grandfather faced the London Missionary Society Directors in 1909 on his second furlough to England, to argue for a mission that equipped the Papuans with the spiritual and practical tools to place them in best stead to play a meaningful part in the future of their country. There was a lot of opposition to missions becoming involved outside of spiritual work, including from the LMS.

To Charles William Abel, with his desire for an industrial mission, his love of work and sport, his love for the Lord, a Christian life was not to be compartmentalized. It applied to all endeavors.

"I did my best to join the Society as a layman; and although I see now, with the Directors, that, all things considered, it was best for me to come among you as a qualified "Reverend", I still strongly protest against my usefulness and influence being limited in any degree by that title. My ordination to the work of a missionary to a savage people should bear with it no disqualification to engage in any necessary work for Christ's sake. Nothing in His Name can secularize me. If I am true to my great trust — the conversion and uplifting of my people — whatever work I touch, to such an end, I spiritualize. I would gladly renounce my ordination so that I might be free to put forth all my energies in Christ's service." **("Charles William Abel of Kwato", Russel W Abel, 1934, pp.105, 106).**

It is from this approach that arose the principles of *"Earua Paisoa"* and *"Nima Paisoa"*, in the Suau language — 'work of the spirit', and 'work of the hand'.

LEADERSHIP IS ABOUT APPLYING THE PRINCIPLES OF LOVE AND SERVICE IN EVERYTHING WE DO.

We may not succeed always, but in the genuine effort towards this intent, we grow spiritually and are rewarded in this physical domain, and beyond it.

I believe that the Lord wants us to serve Him through actually living his Word in the practicality of our daily lives. This is how we best express our faith and our commitment to Him.

If I am to sing praises and worship every day, but live a life divorced from the principles that I am singing about, then I have missed the point entirely.

By the time the legendary civil rights activist, Reverend Martin Luther King Jr. arrived in Memphis, Tennessee, on the 3rd of April 1968, he had been receiving all kinds of death threats because of his activism for black rights. King had previously been stabbed, firebombed, and arrested on numerous occasions. At the end of his speech in Memphis he said,

"Like anybody, I would like to live a long life. Longevity has its place. But I'm not concerned about that now. I just want to do God's will. And He's allowed me to go up to the mountain. And I've looked over. And I have seen the promised land. I may not get there with you. But I want you to know tonight, that we, as a people, will get to the promised land!

And so, I'm happy tonight. I'm not worried about anything. I'm not fearing any man. Mine eyes have seen the glory of the coming of the Lord."

He was shot and killed the next day, April 4th 1968, 6:01 p.m.

Nelson Mandela.

Dr. Frank Buchman.

Rev. Martin Luther King Jr.

Chapter 22

The Meaning of Life

"Waste no more time arguing what a good man should be. Be one." **(Marcus Aurelius, Roman Emperor 161 – 180 AD, and Stoic philosopher).**

"Only a life lived in the service of others is worth living." **(Albert Einstein, theoretical physicist, 1879 – 1955).**

1. Start with the Truth and the Word

There is a universal truth and 'logos' (the divine reason implicit in the cosmos, ordering it and giving it form and meaning), that starts with the principles of the message that the Bible is trying to communicate. It reveals the divine order and truth of love and goodness emanating from a higher power.

Our time in this physical world is a stage of the journey towards the higher power, by meaningfully aspiring and working to do right and rise above the yearnings of the self, through discipline.

Through the exercise of our free will we make conscious choices, learn lessons, and grow.

Without the acknowledgement of this Truth man designs his own truths and unnecessary confusion, and suffering occurs.

The truth is an all-encompassing requirement throughout life in the most fundamental sense. We have to make decisions on the objective truth, not through our political lenses, or personal biases or desire about how we would like the circumstances to be.

The sooner you can make an objective assessment of your own circumstances and abilities, the earlier you can make constructive decisions to turn yourself into the most productive unit possible.

2. Sort yourself out first.

Your first responsibility is to yourself. You cannot contribute to the world if you cannot even look after yourself. This contribution varies for everybody. It's about being the BEST YOU CAN BE, or just as importantly, TRYING TO BE THE BEST YOU CAN BE.

3. Begin your journey as early as possible (time is precious).

Education is key. Appreciate that, and work your butt off to go as far as possible down that path. If the traditional education path is out of your reach you may have to pursue through other means such as on-the-job training.

Start saving as early as possible. Time is the key variable in the establishment of financial security. And NO, money is not the objective, but being responsible for yourself is, and putting yourself into a position where you are helping others, not being a burden on them.

4. Invest in your health.

Understand the gift that God has given you, in your body. Understand the important lessons that discipline over your body, through exercise and diet, can teach. Take pride in the way you look. Appreciate your health while you have it, not after it is gone.

5. All things of value require hard work and discipline.

Nothing that is unearned will be appreciated or valued like something for which you have worked and sacrificed. It is through hard work with a good heart that great things are achieved. These things will last forever and bring true peace and satisfaction.

6. Don't rush into marriage, marry for the right reasons, and work at it every day.

Marriage is sacred and precious. It is the most important relationship in your life. Treat it as such. Not every marriage works out, but if you marry for the right reasons, if you are truly committed to the happiness of your best friend, it will only get better every day.

7. When children come into the world you become the second priority.

These are innocent little people who you have made. Surround them with stability and love. They will give you ten times the love in return and make you so proud.

8. Don't focus on money or possessions, rather, on serving others through creating value.

If your focus is how to help people, the blessings, including material wealth, will flow as a consequence.

9. Blessings flow to those who commit to the spiritual journey and restraint of the flesh.

We are blessed with a physical body and the joys and pain it brings to us, but we need to manage our Lust (sex), Gluttony (food), Sloth (laziness), Greed, Pride, Anger, Envy and Malevolence (desire to do harm to others), and not be directed by them.

10. Responsible love means saying no sometimes.

True love also means tough love at times. People you have relationships with need to be confronted sometimes in their best interest, or in the interest of a healthy relationship.

11. When you commit to something, give it 110 percent.

Everybody values and appreciates a hard worker who is trying his or her best. Your teacher, boss, or spouse will never let you go!

12. Walk the talk.

Do it, then talk about it, not before.

13. Become the champion for good, that you are.

You are a good person, so be the Superman or Superwoman that this world needs more of. Everything hinges on good leadership, and good leadership applies at all levels.

14. Go forward, and courage and conviction will be rewarded.

Nothing was, or will be achieved by sitting at home, talking or dreaming. Make a plan and get on with it. If you fail, try again.

15. Choose to find joy in everyday moments.

Struggles are a part of life, but there are so many blessings to be grateful for. Choose to find joyful moments every day. In the end there is only the sprinkles of love you leave behind.

Kwato Island, 23rd April 2022.

Kwato Island, 23rd April 2022.

Aaliyah Courtney Solomon, a sixth generation Abel,
Independence Day 2022.

ADDENDUM 1

Papua New Guinea Mineral and Petroleum Resource Projects Summary

Edie Creek has been an historic gold and silver mining area since its discovery in 1926. Located about five km south-west of Wau, it was the centre of one of the first major gold rushes in PNG before the Second World War. Large amounts of gold have been extracted by both alluvial and underground mining. Two brothers, William and Stanley Royal found gold at Edie Creek in 1926. On 16 July 1951, a Qantas Drover aircraft crashed into the sea near Lae carrying gold belonging to the Bulolo Gold Dedging Company. It is believed that £35 000 worth of gold bullion was on board. It was recovered later by special divers.

The discovery of vast copper ore deposits in Bougainville's Crown Prince Range led to the establishment of the copper mine in 1969 by **Bougainville Copper Ltd**, a subsidiary of the Australian company, Conzinc Rio Tinto. The mine began production in 1972, with the support of the Papua New Guinea Government, as a 20 percent shareholder. The site was, at the time, the world's largest open-pit copper/gold mine, which generated 12 percent of PNG's GDP and more than 45 percent of the nation's export revenue.

The mine caused devastating environmental damage on the island, and the company was responsible for poisoning the entire length of the Jaba River, which caused birth defects, as well as the extinction of the flying fox on the island.

There was an uprising in 1988, led by Francis Ona, who was a Panguna landowner and commander of the Bougainville Revolutionary Army (BRA). The outcome of the uprising was the Bougainville conflict, between the BRA, who sought secession from PNG, and the Papua New Guinea Defence Force. The ten-year conflict resulted in more than 20 000 deaths, as well as the eventual closure of the mine on 15 May 1989, and the complete withdrawal of BCL personnel by 24 March 1990. It remains closed to this day.

From 1971 to 1989, Bouganville Copper produced three million tonnes of copper, 306 tonnes of gold and 784 tonnes of silver, worth K5.2 billion at the time. This represented 44 percent of PNG's exports over that period, and contributed 17 percent of government revenue.

PNG relied heavily on Panguna before and after Independence. One could argue that the converse is now true now with the heavy reliance by Bouganville on the national purse since the closure of the mine.

OK Tedi Mining Limited (OTML) commenced mining operations in 1984, initially as a gold mine to exploit the gold-rich cap on the Mt. Fubilan deposit, and then as a copper-gold mine in 1987 for the bulk of the ore body.

To 2018, the mine produced five million tonnes of copper, 425 tonnes of gold and 936 tonnes of silver, and generated over 21 billion Kina in revenue. *(MD/CEO Peter Graham, 27 August 2019, The National).*

In 2002, BHP exited OTML, vesting its interest to the Papua New Guinea Sustainable Development Program (PNGSDP).

In 2012, OTML became a fully owned Papua New Guinea company when Inmet Mining Corporation shares were bought out by OTML.

In 2013, OTML became a state-owned enterprise, when the PNGSDP shares were cancelled, and the Government of PNG increased its direct ownership to 87.8 percent.

Originally, the mine was planned to close in 2010. However, following an extensive community consultation process and revised mine plans, the mine life was extended to 2025.

The Porgera Gold Mine is a large gold mining operation located in Enga Province. It began production in 1990 and was developed and operated by Placer Dome, which was acquired in 2006 by Barrick Gold, the world's largest gold mining company at that time. Emperor Gold Mine, which held a minority stake of 20 percent, was sold to Barrick in April 2007.

This gave Barrick (Niugini) a 95 percent ownership of the operation. The remaining five percent is owned by Mineral Resources Enga (MRE) – the landowners, and the Enga Provincial Government. Barrick Gold Corporation and Zijin Mining Group each own 50 percent of Barrick (Niugini) Ltd.

In 2020, the Papua New Guinea Government decided not to renew Barrick Gold's lease on the mine, prompting Barrick to sue the Government within Papua New Guinea, and at an international tribunal. The Government backed down after negotiating a greater ownership stake in the joint venture.

The mine employs more than 3 300 Papua New Guineans. It has produced some 567 tonnes of gold up to 2017, and has contributed approximately ten percent of PNG's total annual exports.

The Porgera Gold Mine is yet to be reopened following the mining lease renewal issues in 2020.

Misima Island is located 625 km east of Port Moresby in the Solomon Sea. Gold was discovered on the island in 1888 with small-scale underground mining continuing until the Second World War. Placer Dome Inc (Placer) commenced exploration in 1977, with production beginning in 1989. Misima was operated as an open-pit gold mine from 1989 to 2004, producing 118 tonnes of gold.

Kingston Resources is working on reopening the Misima Mine against a projected 112 tonnes of gold in reserves.

The **Lihir** Mine is an open-cut gold mine that is operating on Lihir Island in the Bismarck Archipelago. It is wholly owned by Newcrest Mining.

The Lihir Gold Mine is expected to become a one-million ounces-plus gold producer for at least a decade from financial year 2024.

The gold mine was managed by a subsidiary of Rio Tinto until late 2005, and the operatorship was then handed over to Lihir Gold. Australian miner Newcrest Mining acquired Lihir Gold in a AUD $9 billion deal in 2010.

In February 2008, Lihir Gold announced that it would proceed with a major upgrade to the mine, lifting gold production by an annual average of 240 000 ounces over the life of the operation. This equates to an increase in output from 2011 to 2021, to more than 283 tonnes.

Lihir employs approximately 4 500 residential and fly-in-fly-out workers.

Hidden Valley is an open-pit gold-silver mine that is located in Morobe Province of Papua New Guinea. Construction of the mine started in 2007 and commercial production began in September 2010. The mine has an initial life estimate of fourteen years and currently has approximately 2 000 employees.

Newcrest and Harmony Gold Mining of South Africa own the mine through a 50/50 joint-venture (JV) called Hidden Valley JV (HVJV), which is one of three JVs between Newcrest Mining and Harmony Gold, collectively known as the Morobe Mining JVs (MMJV). As of 1 January 2022, the Hidden Valley extension project in Papua New Guinea will be self- funded and will extend the life of the mine for five years to 2027. The company expects the project to deliver approximately six tonnes of gold and 71 tonnes of silver per annum. Over a 14-year life, this will yield 84 tonnes of gold and 994 tonnes of silver.

The **Simberi Gold Mine** is located on Simberi Island in the Tabar Islands Group, New Ireland Province of Papua New Guinea. The mine lies approximately 60 km north-west of the Lihir Gold Project.

Commercial production at the Simberi open-pit mine commenced in 2008. The mine has 69 tonnes of gold reserves.

St Barbara acquired the Allied Gold Mining Company in September 2012, and fully owns the Simberi mine. The mine is expected to have a life of nine years and currently employs approximately 700 employees.

The US$ 2.1 billion Ramu **Nickel Project,** that integrates mining, beneficiation and refining, is located near Madang, on the north coast of Papua New Guinea. It is one of the largest and most ambitious mining and processing projects to have been successfully brought into production in PNG. It comprises laterite open-pit mining, a 135 kilometre slurry pipeline, high pressure acid leaching, deep-sea tailings placement (DSTP), as well as a number of supporting facilities. The project produces nickel/cobalt intermediate product, in which the aggregate nickel metal accounts for 31 000 tonnes per year and cobalt 3 000 tonnes per year. The project has proven reserves of 21 million tons of cobalt at 0.1 percent grade and 21 million tonnes of nickel at 0.91 percent grade. It has a mine life of fourteen years, as of 2019.

Newcrest Mining Limited and Harmony Gold Mining Company Limited each own 50 percent of the **Wafi-Golpu Project** through the Wafi- Golpu Joint Venture (WGJV). The Wafi-Golpu Project is an advanced exploration project located in the Morobe Province of Papua New Guinea, some 65 kilometres south-west of Lae City.

The WGJV has applied for a Special Mining Lease for the Wafi-Golpu Project and has submitted an Environment Impact Statement to the PNG Government that is currently undergoing a regulatory review process. The project has estimated reserves of 622 tonnes of gold.

The **Frieda River Project** is a proposed large open-cast mine and associated infrastructure in the Sandaun and East Sepik Provinces of Papua New Guinea. The mine is located along a tributary of the Sepik River. The deposit is a large copper-gold porphyry deposit. The project includes a hydroelectric scheme to provide electricity and the proposed Frieda River Airport. In 2010, the mine had estimated reserves of 445 tonnes of gold.

The project was originally majority owned by Xstrata. It is now owned 80 percent by Chinese state-owned PanAust Ltd after it was bought from Glencore/Xstrata in 2013, and 20 percent by Australian Stock Exchange-listed Highlands Pacific.

PanAust Ltd. is an Australian incorporated company owned by Guangdong Rising H.K. Limited, which is a wholly owned subsidiary of Guangdong Rising Assets Management Co. Ltd, which is a Chinese state-owned company in Guangdong Province, China.

Other smaller mines include Kainantu Gold Mine, Mt. Kare, Woodlark Gold, and the prospective Solwara 1 Project.

Kutubu Oil was Papua New Guinea's first commercial oil project. Discovered in 1986 in the Southern Highlands Province.

Kutubu crude comprised blended crude from the Kutubu, Moran and Gobe Main and South East Gobe oil fields.

Commercial production commenced in 1992 with a maximum production of 139 000 bbls/day in 1993.

Production has since declined and is now producing at an average of 6 000 bbls/day.

The main project operator was Oil Search Limited (now Santos) in partnership with the landowner companies.

With the commencement of LNG production in May 2014, LNG has overtaken gold as the number one export commodity.

The **PNG LNG Project** is an integrated development that includes gas production and processing facilities which extend from Hela, Southern Highlands, Western, and Gulf Provinces to Port Moresby, the capital city of PNG.

ExxonMobil PNG Limited (33.2 percent interest) is the operator of PNG LNG on behalf of its co-venture partners. The co-venture partners are; Oil Search Limited (OSL) 29 percent interest*, Kumul Petroleum Holdings Limited 16.8 percent interest, Santos Limited 13.5 percent interest, JX Nippon Oil & Gas Exploration 4.7 percent interest and Mineral Resource Development Company Limited (MRDC) with 2.8 percent interest.

The LNG facilities are connected by more than 700 kilometres of onshore and offshore pipeline, and include a gas conditioning plant in Hides and a liquefaction and storage facility near Port Moresby. LNG production began in April 2014, and since then the operator has been supplying LNG to four long-term major customers in the Asia region. The customers include, China Petroleum and Chemical Corporation (Sinopec), Osaka Gas Company Ltd, The Tokyo Electric Power Company Inc, and CPC Corporation.

In 2017, some 8.3 million tonnes of LNG was produced, which was an increase of 20 percent from the original design specification of 6.9 million tonnes per annum. It is anticipated that the PNG LNG Project will produce an estimate of more than 11 trillion cubic feet of LNG over the life (20 plus years) of the project.

The Papua LNG is a liquefied natural gas (LNG) production project led by Total Energies. Papua LNG started with a significant gas discovery located within the Gulf Province, the Elk-Antelope field. Elk was discovered in 2006 by Elk-1 and Antelope was discovered in 2007 by Elk-4, with an estimated 6.2 to 7.5 trillion cubic feet of gas.

The field lies south of the Bismarck Range mountains. It is approximately 120 kilometres inland from the township of Kerema, and 360 kilometres north-west of Port Moresby, the capital city and major industrial centre, and is now referred to as PRL15.

The gas will supply four electric liquefaction trains (two new and two existing) with a combined capacity of 5.6 million tonnes per annum (Mtpa) over a production life of fifteen years.

The two new trains of production will be constructed within the fence of the existing PNG LNG, to maximise the synergies.

Papua LNG will include nine production wells and a gas processing plant, a 320 kilometre pipeline, 260 kilometres of which will be offshore - as well as liquefaction units in Port Moresby.

It is an approximately US$13 billion project and is scheduled to start construction in 2027 following at least three years of delays.

The P'nyang gas field is located 130 kilometres north-west of Hides, the main PNG LNG field in PNG's Highlands Region.

The aim is for P'nyang to share infrastructure with the PNG LNG project, including its 700 kilometre pipeline and the LNG Plant at Caution Bay, near Port Moresby. However, the Government has been determined to treat P'nyang as a stand-alone project for the purposes of licensing and permitting.

While this may be so, it will be several years before the construction of P'nyang commences. Works on the project are being deliberately phased to commence once the Total-led Papua LNG Project in Gulf Province is complete.

The field contains an estimated 4.4 trillion cubic feet (tcf) of natural gas.

The participants in the P'nyang project are currently ExxonMobil (36.86 percent), Oil Search (36.86 percent)*, Santos (14.3 percent) and JX Nippon affiliate Merlin Petroleum Company (11.96 percent).

Assuming that a gas agreement is finally reached, PNG's national oil company, Kumul Petroleum Holdings Ltd, will acquire a 32.5 percent interest in the project, with the interests of the other participants reducing proportionally.

There are other minor 'stranded' fields in the Western Province. The **Pasca Project** is a small offshore oil project in the Gulf Province.

ADDENDUM 2

The Santiago Principles

The Santiago Principles, or formally the **Sovereign Wealth Funds: Generally Accepted Principles and Practices** (**GAPP**) are designed as a common global set of 24 voluntary guidelines that assign best practices for the operations of Sovereign Wealth Funds (SWFs). They are a consequence of the concern of investors and regulators to establish management principles which address the inadequate transparency, independence, and governance in the industry. They are guidelines to be followed by sovereign wealth fund management to maintain a stable global financial system, proper controls around risk, regulation, and a sound governance structure.

As of 2016, thirty funds have formally signed up to the principles and joined the International Forum of Sovereign Wealth Funds (IFSW), representing collectively 80 percent of assets that are managed by sovereign funds globally, which is US$ 5.5 trillion.

The principles are maintained and promoted by the (IFSWF), whose members have to either have implemented, or aspire to implement, the principles

In 2008, there was growing concern by investors and regulators about SWFs, partially because of their visibility, accountably, and the governance structure. To address these concerns, a joint effort between the International Monetary Fund (IMF) and the "International Working Group of Sovereign Wealth Funds" (IWG-SWF), which represented the coming together of fourteen principle funds including some of the largest, such as GIC Private Limited and Abu Dhabi Investment Authority. The IWG-SWF then drafted the 24 Santiago Principles, to set out common international standards regarding transparency, independence, and governance which SWFs might follow. These principles were made public after being presented to the IMF's International Monetary Financial Committee on 11 October 2008

The twenty-four Santiago Principles state that SWFs need to have the following qualities and attributes:

1. A sound legal framework.
2. A well-defined mission.
3. Domestic activities coordinated with fiscal and monetary authorities.
4. Clearly defined rules for drawdowns.
5. Transparency to the owner.
6. Clear division of roles.
7. Governing bodies appointed in a predetermined manner.
8. Governing bodies that act in the best interest of the SWF.

9. Independence.
10. Formal definition of accountability.
11. Annual reporting.
12. Independent auditors.
13. Ethics and professionalism.
14. Rules-based outsourcing.
15. Ability to abide by rules of foreign countries.
16. Operational independence from the owner.
17. Public transparency.
18. Clear investment policies.
19. Commercial orientation.
20. Restrictions against using privileged information.
21. Shareholder rights policies.
22. Effective risk management.
23. Proper reporting of performance.
24. Regular reviews to ensure its compliance with foregoing Santiago Principles.

References

Books

Abel, Charles W, 1900. *Savage Life in New Guinea*. London, London Missionary Society.

Abel, Chris, 2013. *Ta alina Suau*. Alotau, C. Abel.

Abel, Mary K, 1957. *Charles W. Abel – Papuan Pioneer*. London, Oliphant.

Abel, Russell W, 1934. *Charles William Abel of Kwato, Forty Years in Dark Papua*. New York, Revell.

Anderson, Nicholas, 2018. *The Battle of Milne Bay 1942*. (Australian Army Campaigns Series Book 24.

Basket, Geoff, 1991. *Islands and Mountains*.

Beavis, Halliday, 1994. *My Life In Papua 1929–1967*, Templestowe, Victoria, D.S and R.J Beavis.

Griffin, James (Editor), 1978. *Papua New Guinea Portraits – The Expatriate Experience*. Canberra, Australian National University Press.

Howard, Peter, 1961. *Frank Buchman's Secret*. London, Heinemann.

Lutton, Nancy, 1979. *Larger Than Life: A Biography of Charles Abel of Kwato*. Unpublished MA thesis, University of Papua New Guinea.

Maxwell, John C, 2007. *The 21 Irrefutable Laws of Leadership*. 10th Edition, Nashville, Thomas Nelson.

Monckton, Charles Arthur Whitmore, 1922. *Some Experiences of a New Guinea Resident Magistrate*, USA, Library of Alexandria.

Ritchie, Johnathan, 2012. *Ebia Olewale: A Life of Service,* University of Papua New Guinea Press.

Wedega, Alice (Dame), 1981. *Listen My Country*. A Wedega, Sydney, Pacific Publications.

Wetherell, David, 1996. *Charles Abel and the Kwato Mission of Papua New Guinea*, 1891 – 1975. Melbourne University Press.

Articles and Reports

Abel, Cecil, 1967 *"Sorcery and Power: A Papuan Approach"*, Paper at History Research Seminar, University of Papua New Guinea.

Abel, Cecil, 1992. *"The Battle of Milne Bay: Six Key Factors that Helped to Snatch Victory from Defeat.*

Abel, Cecil, (undated). *"The Kunika Story"*.

Abel, Cecil, 1969. *"The Impact of Charles Abel"*, The 2nd Waigani Seminar, History of Melanesia, University of Papua New Guinea. pp. 265–281.

Abel, Cecil, 1987. *"The Kwato Way"*.

Abel, Cecil, (undated). *"The Background And History of Kwato And The Massim Seafarers of The China Straits"*.

Abel, Russell and Mackay, Dermot, (undated). *"They Broke Their Spears"*.

"Accident Investigation Report, Special Investigation Report 70-5", *1971*. Air Safety Investigation Branch, Department of Civil Aviation Australia, April 1971.

Forster, Robert, 2018. *"Getting the Numbers: How Somare won the 1972 Election"*, PNG Attitude, 28 July 2018

Global Capital Asia, 2018. *"Global Capital Asia, Capital Markets Awards 2018: Bonds"*, 11 December 2018.

IWGSWF, 2008. *"Santiago Principles"*, International Working Group Of Sovereign Wealth Funds, October 2008.

Langmore, Diane, 1972. *"Goaribari, 1904"*, Journal of the Papua New Guinea Society, Vol.6, No.2.

Masurina Limited, *Annual Reports*, 1984, 1989, 1990, 1992, 1993, 1994, 1995, 1997, 1998, 1999, 2001, 2002.

National Planning Department, 2014. *National Strategy for Responsible Sustainable Development, 2nd Edition*. Waigani: Department of National Planning.

Overland, Chris, 2020. *"The Tragic History of Goaribari Island"*, PNG Attitude, 11 April 2020.

Parliamentary Papers, 1907. *"Report of the Royal Commission on the Affray at Goaribari Island, British New Guinea, on the 6th of March 1904."*, Parliamentary Papers, Vol.1, 1907.

Quinn, John *"The Curious Case of Christopher Robinson"*, Papua New Guinea Association of Australia, 21st October 2018.

Treasury Department, 2020. *"The Extractive Industries Transparency Initiative Report 2020"*, PNG Extractive Industries Transparency Initiative, National Secretariat, Department of Treasury.

The National, 2013. *"PNG's First Bond Issue Receives Top Review"* – National Newspaper 14 December, 2018.

Wetherell, David, 1986. *"An Elite for a Nation? Refelections on a Missionary Group in Papua New Guinea, 1890 – 1986"*, Pacific Studies Vol. 9, No. 2, March 1986.

Wetherell, David, 2021. *Abel, Sir Cecil Charles* (1903–1994), Australian Dictionary of Biography, Vol. 19, 2021.

Letters

Abel, Beatrice, 1907. *To Charles W Abel, 16th March 1907*. Abel Papers, New Guinea Collection, Sir Michael Somare Library, UPNG.

Beavis, Halliday*, 1965. "To All Kwato Friends", 12th September 1965*, informing of Russell Abel's death and funeral.

INDEX